AMERICA
AT WAR

1941-1945
THE HOME FRONT

Text
Clark G. Reynolds

Commissioning Editor
Andrew Preston

Publishing Assistant
Edward Doling

Editorial
Gill Waugh

Design
Sally Strugnell

Photography
United Press International/Bettmann, New York
and National Archives, Washington, D.C.

Picture Research
Leora Kahn

Production
Ruth Arthur
David Proffit
Sally Connolly

Director of Production
Gerald Hughes

Director of Publishing
David Gibbon

CLB 2364
This edition first published in the United States 1990 by Gallery Books,
an imprint of W.H. Smith Publishers, Inc.,
112 Madison Avenue, New York, New York 10016.
© 1990 Archive Publishing,
a division of Colour Library Books Ltd., Godalming, Surrey, England.
Printed and bound in Italy.
All rights reserved.
ISBN 0 8317 0300 8

Gallery Books are available for bulk purchase for sales promotions and
premium use. For details write or telephone the Manager of Special Sales,
W.H. Smith Publishers, Inc., 112 Madison Avenue, New York, New York
10016. (212) 532-6600

AMERICA AT WAR

1941-1945
THE HOME FRONT

CLARK G. REYNOLDS

GALLERY BOOKS
An Imprint of W. H. Smith Publishers Inc.
112 Madison Avenue
New York City 10016

AMERICA AT WAR

The nation of immigrants was jolted by the September 2, 1939 headlines announcing the Nazi invasion of Poland the day before. These boys of New York City's Polish district could only wonder at the fate of their relatives left behind in the "Old Country" to be bombed by Hitler's Luftwaffe. The late summer weather has them out-of-doors to read the evening tabloid, but attired according to their mothers' interpretations of the weather: the lad in short pants has a long-sleeved shirt, whereas the one in long trousers has sleeves rolled up; the other two wear knickers and long socks. Shoes are oxfords and sneakers, high and low-ankled.

"To make the world safe for democracy" is the phrase President Woodrow Wilson used to explain the entry of the United States into World War I in 1917. In spite of the victory of the democratic powers in that European conflict, however, few thinking Americans by 1939 deluded themselves into believing democracy had really been saved. In the face of German Naziism, Italian fascism, Japanese imperialism, and Russian Communism, democracy's back was against the wall again. Once persuaded, in 1941, to rescue the European democracies for the second time, the American people meant to settle the matter once and for all. Their fight – at home and overseas – against the Axis dictatorships took on a crusading zeal of fashioning a better world in which democracy could permanently flourish. Their democratic ideals and generosity guided the Allies to victory and provided the model which would take the rest of the planet another half-century to emulate.

World War II was a pivotal period in the history of the human race, but especially for the United States. Down to World War I the great powers of Europe had dominated the globe, though leaving the Pacific basin and East Asia generally to the emerging giants around its rim – the United States, Japan, and China. The conflict of 1914-18 had dealt a mortal blow to the old European empires of Great Britain, France, Germany, and tsarist Russia, but thanks to America's eventual intervention democratic Britain and France had been saved to dictate a new peace in Europe. The visionary Wilson had orchestrated the creation of the international League of Nations in 1919, but a disinterested American public and Congress had refused to let America join. They preferred to let the British and French deter new aggressors, a trust the United States continued even when Hitler's Germany invaded Poland in September 1939 to renew the struggle of 1914-18.

Naive and still innocent in the ways of international power balances, the American people believed themselves superior to a decadent, dying Europe and thus able to remain aloof from events there. It was less an attitude of isolationism than of unilateralism. That is, Americans were perfectly willing to make money from trade with other nations – and to frolic in faraway playgrounds for those who could afford it. But, they had no intention of ever tying America's future and fortunes to allies or any international association like the League. We would never surrender our freedom to act alone. This attitude was reinforced by America's historic and real isolation – a geographic one. The Atlantic "moat" protected our shores from European invaders even if Britain and France collapsed, and the Monroe Doctrine kept foreign interlopers out of the American hemisphere. If Europe persisted in committing suicide in another war, America always had the refuge of remaining neutral. And the growing range of multi-engine bombing aircraft during the 1930s could be ignored through similar wishful thinking.

The Pacific Ocean was another matter. For, vast as it is, no British Isles or Royal Navy stood between California and the truculent empire of Japan which had defeated China in 1895 and tsarist Russia ten years later. During America's own brief flirtation with territorial imperialism at that time, the nation had acquired a thin string of islands from Hawaii to the Philippines and had become the staunch defender of the national sovereignty of a feeble China, then struggling to enter the modern world. The bold cruise of President Teddy Roosevelt's "Great White Fleet" of sixteen battleships across the Pacific in 1908 had impressed imperial Japan, but post-World War I America had no stomach for the ensuing arms race with Japan, a competition it arrested by battleship limitation treaties at Washington in 1922 and London in 1930. Unwilling, however, to keep the fleet up to the levels allowed by these agreements – like Japan did – the U.S. government had relied on moral persuasion to keep the peace in the Pacific, notably the Kellogg-Briand pact of 1927 which had called for the outlawing of war.

Firmly rooted in the ethical principles of English democratic institutions and international law, the American people took a dim view of aggression of any kind. But their stomachs came first, and the Great Depression which began in 1929 quickly permeated all aspects of

American life. So Presidents Herbert Hoover and Franklin D. Roosevelt respectively could do nothing more than protest Japan's invasion of Manchuria in 1931 and its general attack on China in 1937. Neither could Adolf Hitler's and Benito Mussolini's acquisitions in Europe and North Africa be countered beyond mere words by an increasingly concerned FDR. His New Deal relief programs and economic reforms understandably commanded the attention of the average American. If democracy and capitalism could not survive at home – and many far left intellectuals doubted they could – then what chance could they have abroad? Charity had to begin here.

The fact was, however, that the United States had become a global industrial and trading power whose political, economic, and social well-being depended on a world in which it did not stand alone. America relied absolutely on the ability to engage in peaceful trading relationships. But of all the institutions in the country during the interwar years, only one of them fully appreciated this reality – the U.S. Navy. The several Presidents, Congress, and the State and War Departments, including the U.S. Army and its Air Corps, shared the public's opinion in the 1920s and 1930s that the country should focus its defenses on the Western Hemisphere and even withdraw from the war-torn western Pacific. The U.S. Army was a small professional service oriented primarily to coast defense; it had been enlarged with volunteers only twice in its history to fight major conflicts – the Civil War and World War I. The Navy, on the other hand, was steeped in the global theories of its turn-of-the-century philosopher-historian Alfred Thayer Mahan: the Navy should be brought up to treaty strength in order to protect American commerce in the Pacific, defend the Philippines, and preserve China. Only by doing this could Japan be deterred or, if need be, defeated in wartime. Maritime America had to be defended on the other side of the Pacific – and in the Atlantic – if her free-trade prosperity and free institutions were to continue.

Franklin Roosevelt understood this strategic reality but could do little to strengthen the Navy or Army without public support. Congress passed neutrality laws in 1935 and 1937 restricting the sale of arms to nations at war, while well-publicized hearings led by Senator Gerald Nye had pointed the finger of guilt for World War I at munitions manufacturers. Peace-loving Americans, they argued, should not be party to foreign wars, either through arms sales, collective security pacts, or outright participation. Even unilateral rearmament meant a threat to American political freedoms, reasoned the advocates of outright isolationism, and FDR had no choice but to tread softly over the question of preparing the country for war.

The German attack on Poland on September 1, 1939 began World War II and gave the President his first opportunity to prepare the United States for probable entry into it. Although at least half the American public sensed no urgency, FDR used his executive authority to form a neutrality patrol in the Atlantic on the 5th, two days after Britain and France declared war on Germany. On the 8th he declared a "limited national emergency" and extended the air and ship neutrality patrols into the Caribbean and Philippine waters, thus allowing British and French forces there to return home. By the end of the month, he had convinced the Latin American states to join the United States in creating a mutual 300-mile hemispheric "safety belt" against the belligerents. (Canada was already at war as part of the British Commonwealth.) And in November he persuaded Congress to revise the neutrality laws to permit the sale of weapons to foreign powers on a "cash and carry" basis. Of course, this market would be open only to the democratic Allies, who immediately placed large orders for aircraft and their engines with American companies. FDR charged Secretary of the Treasury Henry Morganthau with coordinating the sales.

Though the American public did not realize it, these actions subtly brought the United States into World War II. At first the hostilities became a "phony war," since neither Germany nor the Allies made major moves over the winter of 1939-40, leading Americans into a sense of complacency. The actions of the Soviet Union, however, elicited American sympathy for victims of oppression: Poland, which was divided up between

AMERICA AT WAR

Germany and Russia, and Finland, which Russia crushed in March 1940. A nonaggression pact between Hitler and Joseph Stalin had made these events possible and, incidentally, had thereby undermined Communist sympathizers in the United States. Congress and the people debated what action to take, but the vague neutrality policy prevented most segments of American society from feeling any sense of urgency.

Suddenly, on April 9, 1940 Germany launched a massive *blitzkrieg*, lightning war, against Denmark and Norway, followed in May by Belgium, the Netherlands and France. As these nations fell one by one to the Nazi juggernaut, shock waves of alarm swept across America. Though Roosevelt hesitated in confronting the strong isolationist elements in Congress, Representative Carl Vinson, Chairman of the House Naval Affairs Committee, knew better. Already working on a naval expansion bill since January, he quickly devised a program calling for 15,000 new naval aircraft and convinced FDR it would pass. Thus encouraged, the President seized the initiative and surprised Congress, the Army, and the Navy on May 16 by calling for the production of 50,000 military aircraft a year. Few people objected, for now the *Wehrmacht* pinned the British Expeditionary Force against the sea at French Dunkirk. The same day that that army began to be evacuated, FDR created the National Defense Research Council (NDAC) to supervise American military-industrial mobilization, and on June 5 he quietly agreed to transfer 50 old Navy dive bombers to France – a clearly unneutral act.

But it was too late for France. On June 10, Mussolini's Italy declared war and invaded France from the east, while the Germans bore down from the north. Congress hurriedly passed Vinson's naval expansion bill on the 15th, the very day that the Germans marched into Paris. Vinson quickly drafted yet another naval bill, which called for a two-ocean navy and sold FDR on it, but France surrendered a week later. This tragedy acted as an elixir to the administration, which now added 14,000 projected aircraft for the British to the 50,000 earmarked for America's armed forces. The two-ocean bill passed easily on July 19, reflecting the government's equal concern over Japan in the Pacific. Indeed, the President had already ordered the Fleet to remain in Hawaii after its annual maneuvers rather than return to its bases along the West coast. Its presence there was designed to deter Japan from expanding its war in China. And on July 25 he placed an embargo on the export of aviation gas and scrap iron and steel to Japan.

Before the summer of 1940, the people of the United States had been preoccupied with returning to the normal life of realizing the American dream. An entire decade of Depression had not dented the unemployment figure of over 9,000,000 people, but Roosevelt's New Deal had stressed action, experimentation, fiscal responsibility, and even social security. Business was booming again, and hard physical and legal battles by organized labor had made the unions into potent guarantors of the average worker. A new generation of teenagers had propelled the young forward to the jumping beat of jazz-inspired swing bands, while Hollywood and radio provided welcome escape and fantasy. During the Christmas season of 1939 alone the films *Gone With the Wind* and *The Wizard of Oz* had capped the biggest year yet for the golden age of American filmmaking. The onset of the war in Europe brought subtle changes in popular musical tastes, however, with the young starting to turn toward the less-frenetic, romantic sounds of the Glenn Miller Orchestra. The living room radio had a more direct influence, as Edward R. Murrow reported live the German bombings of London.

Public sympathy for the victims of the Nazi scourge mounted and with it Roosevelt's assertive leadership to strengthen not only America's defenses but Britain's as well. He had no preconceived plan, nor did he empower others to establish a full-blown wartime mobilization program. He used a trial-and-error approach as he had with the New Deal, and he meant to preserve those social reforms even as he prepared the nation for war. It was a tough balancing act, especially since the Republicans nominated charismatic business leader Wendell Willkie to run against his bid for a third term in November. Luckily for Roosevelt, this opponent shared his pro-British stance, but the vocal isolationists forced him to guarantee American neutrality in the European conflict.

Already commander in chief of the Army and Navy under the Constitution, FDR expanded these powers to include industrial war production. He appointed himself head of the NDAC though delegating the specific tasks to captains of industry, notably General Motors president William S. Knudsen to head production. And when that agency proved inadequate, in January 1941 he replaced the NDAC with the Office of Production Management (OPM) under Knudsen. But FDR hamstrung the aircraft and shipping industries the entire summer of 1940 by insisting that statutory limitations be placed on their profits, lest they engage in war profiteering. A compromise was finally reached in October, but their profits soared anyway. Congress allowed him to increase the size of the regular army to 375,000 men, but a national draft was essential to mobilization, leading to a long Congressional debate which resulted in the Selective Service Act on September 16. Empowered now to create an Army of 1,400,000 men, the President thereupon called up the National Guard units of the states to be part of it. He tried to keep a lid on the Navy's expansion for training facilities, but allowed himself to be persuaded by Carl Vinson to raise appropriation levels.

Essential to the efficient management of the nation's mobilization on such an unprecedented scale were skilled administrators like Knudsen. To run the two major defense agencies, the Departments of War and the Navy, over the summer Roosevelt brought in two Republicans favorable to his interventionist policy. For Secretary of War, he chose Henry L. Stimson, who had held the job three decades before and been Secretary of State under Hoover. For the Navy, he selected newspaperman Frank Knox. But for their lieutenants, who would actually reorganize the military for war, he chose brilliant managers from the corporate, legal, and banking sectors, notably James V. Forrestal and Robert P. Patterson, under secretaries of the Navy and War respectively. By such measures Roosevelt was creating a war cabinet and diffusing partisan politics, as revealed in November when he handily defeated Willkie at the polls.

Concurrently, the President sought ways to bolster the British defense against Germany with emergency help, since American industry would take at least two years and probably three to tool up to the projected capacity. Timetables would also be affected by whenever the United States would be dragged into the shooting. One major scheme FDR promoted was to trade 50 World War I-vintage destroyers to the British navy for use against German submarines in return for long-term American utilization of British bases in the Western Hemisphere for shoring up America's naval and air defenses. This destroyers-for-bases deal was concluded on September 2, giving the U.S. access to Bermuda, Canadian Newfoundland, and several Caribbean islands. But two days later vocal isolationist business leaders and politicians formed the American First Committee to lobby against the country's drift toward war. Most prominent of them was the famous aviator Charles Lindbergh, who, as the first person to fly solo eastward across the Atlantic in 1927, was suitably impressed that the German *Luftwaffe* might do the same in the other direction if America entered the war.

As the Battle of Britain raged in the skies over southern England and London in mid-1940, Roosevelt strengthened American ties with the former mother country and personally with its resolute prime minister, Winston Churchill. Both countries initiated exchanges of military experts for informal discussions which led to formal talks in Washington early in 1941. Fears of a German invasion of England resulted in a remarkable move by the British to begin sending large numbers of their young children in ocean liners across the U-boat-infested North Atlantic to live with American and Canadian families until, as the song said, "there'll be bluebirds over the white cliffs of Dover...when the world is free." Some 10,000 youngsters made the crossing before 90 perished in a sub attack, causing the British to end the desperate scheme. The presence of these escapees from the Nazi terror fueled American sympathy for Britain; the children remained here for several years.

As American men began to enlist or register for the draft, inexorably upsetting the tenor of American life, any pretence of the potential enemies' friendliness toward the United States was dispelled on September 27, 1940. That day diplomats of Hitler, Mussolini, and Emperor

Hirohito signed the Tripartite Pact, a formal Axis alliance aimed at the United States.

Roosevelt responded on December 20 in a "Fireside Chat" over the radio to the American public in which he proclaimed that the United States would become the "arsenal of democracy." He then proposed that American weapons be provided to Britain and China on a "lend-lease" basis. Instead of saddling these nations with heavy postwar debts, as after World War I, they could borrow the tools of war and return them after the war. The proposed bill – strategically numbered 1776 in the House – evoked a furious debate in Congress, for it meant, in the words of Secretary of War Stimson, nothing less than "economic war" on the Axis powers. While Congress argued, FDR advised his generals and admirals to plan for possible entry into the European war as early as April 1941. Lend-Lease passed on March 11 and would ultimately result in many billions of dollars being directed to the Allies.

Then in May, a German U-boat sank an American freighter, the *Robin Moor*, in the South Atlantic, causing no loss of life but inspiring sufficient indignation by the administration that it froze all German and Italian financial assets and closed all German consulates in the United States. Later in the month the German battleship *Bismarck* broke out into the North Atlantic to attack British merchant shipping, whereupon Roosevelt declared an "unlimited national emergency" and directed American aircraft to search for and report *Bismarck's* movements to the British. The Royal Navy sank her first, but America was now in an undeclared naval war against Germany. In July, U.S. Marines landed in Iceland to relieve the British garrison there, and the U.S. Atlantic Fleet extended its neutrality patrols to escort merchant ships as far as that island, with orders to shoot at hostile German and Italian vessels. The diplomatic tension mounted.

The first line of the Anglo-American effort in 1941 lay in aircraft, causing the previously small U.S. aircraft industry to mushroom into the biggest business in America. To intensify the production and development of strategic bombers for use against Hitler, the U.S. Army upgraded its Air Corps to be the U.S. Army Air Forces (AAF). For warfare at sea in both oceans, the U.S. Navy initiated a program to build large numbers of aircraft carriers and planes; several smaller escort carriers were even turned over to the British under Lend-Lease. During the summer, both American air arms even began training British pilots at U.S. air stations, further bringing Britishers into daily contact with the American people. In July, when Japan occupied French Indochina, Roosevelt froze Japanese financial assets in the United States.

When the *Luftwaffe* failed to defeat the Royal Air Force in the Battle of Britain, Hitler decided against invading England in favor of Russia. In June 1941 the *Wehrmacht* launched its invasion of the Soviet Union, and – although the British and American people had little sympathy for communism and Stalin's attacks on Poland and Finland – their hearts went out to any victims of the Nazis, and Roosevelt extended Lend-Lease to Russia. As for a mounting Japanese offensive in China, the administration gave Army and Navy pilots leave to serve as volunteer "Flying Tiger" fighter pilots for China.

By midsummer of 1941 the United States was becoming not only the arsenal of democracy but an armed camp. Even hard-line isolationists could not dispute the need for the many military training stations and increased weapons procurement, simply because the country had to survive in an increasingly hostile world. Few Americans feared that their nation was imperiled, however. The deeply ingrained notion of America's destiny as the hope of the human race reached as far back as the Pilgrims fleeing Europe and the successful Revolution against Britain. The triumph of American arms in World War I had been proof positive for Americans that Europe was finished as the center of progress. And, in spite of the Depression, the Statue of Liberty had resumed its symbolic beacon for emigrés fleeing Germany ever since Hitler's accession to power in 1933. The New Deal had restored American optimism, and the call to arms to defend our liberty swelled American pride. But whether to become an open ally of Britain and China in the new world war remained the point of issue.

Franklin Roosevelt masterfully met the challenge by wedding traditional American values to the cause of all freedom-loving peoples. That August of 1941 he and Winston Churchill rendezvoused aboard respective warships "somewhere off Maine" announced the White House. But they actually met in a harbor of Canadian Newfoundland – a British Commonwealth territory from which U.S. patrol planes searched daily for Axis submarines. There the two heads of the democratic superpowers articulated the Atlantic Charter, a set of "common principles...for a better future for the world." These were the "Four Freedoms," first announced publicly in January by Roosevelt: freedom of speech, freedom of religion, freedom from fear, and freedom from want. More specifically, the Charter called for political self-determination of oppressed peoples, no more territorial acquisitions by any nation, and open trade for all. In a sense, the Charter was a restatement of Woodrow Wilson's noble internationalist aims of 1919, only this time the democratic leaders were determined to realize them. And in September the administration announced its "Victory Program" to outbuild the Axis in munitions by spending $45 billion a year – a figure soon to be tripled.

All that remained to rally full-fledged American patriotism behind any all-out war effort was the sacrifice of American lives. This nearly happened on September 4 when the U.S. destroyer *Greer* and a U-boat exchanged blows, though to no effect, and on October 17 when the *Kearny* took a torpedo hit which wounded several crewmen. Then, two weeks later, the destroyer *Reuben James* was sunk by a U-boat while escorting an Allied convoy from Newfoundland. Two-thirds of her 159-man crew perished. An outraged Congress immediately repealed the neutrality law which had forbidden open trade with nations at war. This occurred in mid-November, just as two special envoys arrived from Japan to try to resolve the growing deterioration of Japanese-American relations in the Pacific. The country watched and waited anxiously for an extension of the peace in the Pacific even as it drifted into the war in the Atlantic.

Pearl Harbor meant nothing to the average American on December 6, 1941, but it was on everyone's lips the next day. Even when newscaster John Daly reported its location, he misspelled and mispronounced its location on Hawaiian Oahu as "the island of O-ha-u." The announcement of Japan's sneak attack on the U.S. Fleet based there was radio's most dramatic hour. Though the public had been excited by the on-the-spot radio account of the crash of the dirigible *Hindenburg* in 1937, alarmed by Orson Wells' recreation of the Martian invasion in "War of the Worlds" on Halloween night 1938, and sobered by Edward R. Murrow's live accounts of the bombing of London in 1940, nothing prepared the radio audience for that Sunday afternoon bulletin, "We interrupt this program to bring you an important announcement..." America would never again be the same.

In three hours planes from six Japanese aircraft carriers had caught the Fleet completely by surprise and crippled it – just how severely the government would not admit for years. But the loss of life and the general destruction could not be hidden, nor the fact that the Fleet had been so devastated that it would be incapable of counterattacking for a long time to come. "Remember Pearl Harbor" became the rallying cry of the country, and the voice of isolationism died forever. Next day the President made his ringing address about that "day on infamy" before a joint session of Congress, broadcast throughout the land – and Congress declared war. No-one had ever suggested "Remember the *Reuben James*," but Hitler and Mussolini solved that problem by declaring war on the United States on December 11, a move instantly reciprocated. Everything was now official.

"Old Dr. New Deal," FDR remarked at a press conference, must give way to "Dr. Win-the-War," meaning simply that victory over the aggressor nations assumed the highest priority. "Victory" became the catchword behind America's war aims. It was a word which everyone understood. A nation with a unified will to win – the major result of the Pearl Harbor attack – could fight the war absolutely and with a clear direction. Over a century before, the German philosopher of war Karl von Clausewitz had argued that just such national unity was the key ingredient to victory in war. FDR sealed the call to arms by sanctifying it; he proclaimed January

AMERICA AT WAR

1, 1942 as a national day of prayer. "Our strength," he said, "as the strength of all men everywhere, is of greater avail as God upholds us."

Redirecting national energies toward winning a war, but with little thought to a coherent postwar peacetime policy, was typical of all of America's past wars and often those of other nations as well. No-one could doubt that the task of winning World War II would assume Herculean proportions, which thoroughly justified short-sightedness in many of the details and even negligence over long-term aims. And since many public opinion polls during 1942 revealed that nearly half the American people had little actual inkling of "what this war is all about," as one Gallup Poll put it, promoting the war as a moral crusade for simple victory met the nation's immediate needs.

Roosevelt and Churchill expanded their Atlantic Charter and Four Freedoms goals to a broad international scale when the prime minister traveled to Washington two weeks after Pearl Harbor. In discussions with the Commonwealth nations and most Latin American states, they issued the Declaration of the United Nations – officially on January 1, 1942 – in which 26 countries (eventually 46 in all) endorsed the waging of total war on the basis of the Atlantic Charter and not to conclude a separate peace with any of the enemy powers. The American people warmly supported it and thereby, unwittingly, took the first step toward accepting a permanent postwar union of nations.

In the enthusiasm of the early hours of the great struggle, however, a major contradiction began to surface which reflected the fact that only the United States among the great powers was geographically isolated and thus immune from direct physical damage in this war, as had been the case during World War I. On the one hand, Americans could naively declare that the class structures and balances of power typical throughout European history had been a direct cause of Europe's many wars. Henry Luce, scion of the Time, Life, and Fortune magazine publishing giant, observed in 1942 that because the United States was "alone among the nations of the earth...founded on ideas which transcend class and caste

and racial and occupational differences, America alone can provide the pattern for the future" and thus act as "elder brother of the nations in the brotherhood of man." That is, the old European power structure should be dismantled after final victory in favor of American-style democracy.

On the other hand, FDR called for a war of survival in 1942 in order to preserve the prewar status quo of the democracies, meaning the British, French, and Dutch colonial empires in South Asia, Africa, and the Middle East and American hegemony in the Western Hemisphere, presumably to be extended over the Pacific as well. Liberal critics like Vice President Henry A. Wallace and Wendell Willkie saw the contradiction and opted, as Willke said in his 1943 book *One World*, for a global arrangement on the American model. The old European order must go, they said – a direct challenge especially to America's British ally.

Neither did the professed extension of the American dream on a global scale jibe with the wartime realities of making concessions to less-than-democratic regimes in order to achieve victory. To make the Stalinist dictatorship palatable to the American people, Roosevelt had to convince himself and the public that Soviet Russia could be "handled" to achieve postwar cooperation – and the disillusion sufficed in the interest of bringing the full weight of the Red Army against Hitler. To initiate the invasion of North Africa in November 1942, the administration had to court the neutrality of the fascist regime of Francisco Franco in Spain and make a deal with the German Vichy-French North African puppet Admiral François Darlin to change sides after the initial American landings. The latter concession was an affront to the Free French of General Charles de Gaulle, who had escaped to England to continue the fight. In China, the State Department chose to identify the corrupt authoritarian Nationalist government of Generalissimo Chiang Kai-shek as the proper focus of Chinese resistance to Japan, when in fact other warlords and the Chinese Communist Party fought equally hard against the invader – and against Chiang. Even in Latin America – the "good neighbor" that Roosevelt had declared in 1933 – heavy financial support of ruling dictators was justified in the interest of hemispheric military solidarity.

Sensitive to criticism over such compromises to his democratic ideals and determined to better articulate America's war aims, Roosevelt journeyed to North African Casablanca after its liberation, where he met with Churchill in January 1943. There he declared America's goal in the European theater of war (ETO) to be nothing less than the "unconditional surrender" of Nazi Germany. The phrase – borrowed from General U.S. Grant's attack on Ft. Donelson in the Civil War – struck a responsive chord in the American people, who had always preferred such direct and complete solutions in time of war. Returning home, the President informed Congress, "It is clear to us that if Germany and Italy and Japan – or any one of them – remain armed at the end of this war or are permitted to rearm, they will again, and inevitably, embark upon an ambitious career of world conquest."

Such a simplistic indictment of these three peoples smacked strongly of racial overtones, suggesting that, biologically and ethnically, these enemies had aggression in their blood and did not deserve another chance. They were, in short, inherently evil. FDR's evidence was their political and military record over the preceding half-century, a view which in fact represented that of his generation of Americans but hardly provable in the sweep of history, before or since. The postwar world, he argued, should be stripped of war-inducing power balances and regulated by a unilateral police force of peace-loving nations: the United States, Great Britain, the Soviet Union, France, and China. Naive the scheme was, like most American thinking about the rest of the world, but it received its first endorsement in October 1943 when Secretary of State Cordell Hull journeyed to Moscow to sign an agreement with the Russians, British, and Chinese laying the groundwork for what would become the formal United Nations. The next month, following the Allied assaults on Sicily and Italy, the Italians managed to drive out Mussolini's fascists, whereupon FDR happily allowed them to change sides and support the Allies – a quick turnabout in his belief of their inherent aggressiveness.

Such expediencies aside, Roosevelt pressed forward with his war aim of unconditional surrender by extending it to Japan when he met with Churchill and Chiang Kai-shek at Cairo, Egypt, in late-November 1943. He then proceeded to Teheran, Iran, to cement relations with Stalin and assure him of the forthcoming assault by the Western allies on occupied France at Normandy the following spring. Following the June 1944 D-Day landings, Roosevelt and Churchill met in September at Quebec, Canada, to arrange the postwar settlement over Germany. There FDR endorsed

INTRODUCTION

the Morgenthau Plan of his Treasury Secretary to reduce the industrial German state into "a potato patch" of small farms. This truculent attitude had little more to recommend it than simple vengeance, however, and he scotched it a month later. Then Roosevelt, Churchill, and Stalin met at Yalta in the Russian Crimea early in 1945, where they announced that the United Nations would convene in San Francisco that April to forge the postwar world order so long sought by force of Allied arms.

Just as bringing together the disunited and discordant family of nations was essential to defeating the Axis, so too did the melting pot of peoples who comprised the United States have to be welded as one if victory was to be realized. This equally created immediate contradictions, which Willkie, eclipsing many liberals, also spelled out in his book. How could America profess democracy on a global scale if it practiced "imperialism at home," namely, the social and economic subjugation of the Negro race and other minorities? The problem of the blacks was only the oldest and most obvious prejudice of white America. "The yellow peril" of Japan had festered ever since the turn of the century and now played a major role in rallying public opinion to fight "those slant-eyed bastards" who had sneaked up on Pearl Harbor. The extreme anti-German bias during World War I had led even to changing German words for the duration of that war, for example, dachshund into "Liberty hound." At least in this war anti-German feeling could be channeled more toward the Nazi gangsters. But anti-Japanese feeling erupted so violently after December 7, 1941 that anybody Japanese in America was quickly labeled alien and dangerous. The American people began looking for scapegoats for their disaster.

This feeling, as in the past, was centered on the U.S. West coast, where fears of a Japanese invasion were most pointed and fed upon initial (though groundless) government suspicion over "fifth column" saboteurs in Hawaii who might have played a part in the Pearl Harbor attack. At the end of January 1942 an anxious Attorney General Francis Biddle ordered all West coast Japanese, German, and Italian aliens to be moved inland, but without following the Canadian example of placing all its Japanese adult males in work camps in the interior. Then, of all people, the eminent liberal columnist Walter Lippmann succumbed to a growing nervousness and frustration over U.S. defeats in the Pacific by calling for the internment of all Japanese-born Issei and their American-born, citizen Nisei offspring. The paranoic Army commander on the West coast took up Lippmann's idea: "A Jap's a Jap," said he, "It makes no difference if he's an American citizen." Or, "to hell with *habeas corpus* until the danger is over," cried columnist Westbrook Pegler. Legal and military experts countenanced an increasingly hysterical public, and on February 19 Commander in Chief Roosevelt gave the order to remove the Japanese-Americans from the Pacific coast. Four days later, the Japanese submarine I-17 bombarded (ineffectually) an oil field near Santa Barbara, California – a timely affirmation of West coasters' fears for their safety.

The Army allowed voluntary evacuation during March, but made it mandatory when states to the east of California refused to accept the evacuees. Over the next two months the Japanese-Americans were herded into temporary camps, soon replaced by permanent ones – virtual prisons or really concentration camps as FDR unguardedly called them, unaware of the possible similarity between Nazi and American abrogation of the civil liberties of minorities. The Nisei, never given a trial and therefore any hope of pardon, forfeited their homes, businesses, schoolwork, and rights. Their bitterness over the hollowness of the American dream ran deep, and suicides were not unknown. By August more than 100,000 of them had been rounded up – including people with only one Japanese grandparent – and placed under the jurisdiction of a new agency, the War Relocation Authority. Nine camps of about 10,000 occupants each were scattered behind a north-south line 200 or more miles from the coast.

As if prison life were not bad enough, in 1943 the internees were ordered to enhance their required loyalty oath to the United States by rejecting all familial ties with Japan. When 7,000 refused, they were moved to a camp at Tule Lake, California, under maximum guard – where, during a riot at the end of the year, they were brutally crushed by troops.

The greatest proof of their loyalty, however, came the same year when the Army allowed young Nisei men to enlist in their own regimental combat team, the 442nd, which subsequently garnered rich honors for itself in the Italian campaign.

Camp conditions only gradually improved, and during 1944 many Nisei were allowed to leave for points East. The virulent racism of white America subsided, and in 1945 the Nisei and Issei were permitted to begin returning to their California homes. Most had been financially wiped out, some $400 million in all, and though Congress allowed some $30 million of that lost to be made up in individual claims starting in 1948, the victims of relocation and their descendants did not receive across-the-board monetary compensation for their sacrifices until Congress finally authorized such payments in 1989. The wartime treatment of the Nisei was an unmitigated black eye to American democratic principles – and another telling revelation of white America's naiveté toward the wider world.

One fact of democratic states throughout modern history, however, is that civil liberties have been suspended in wartime when national security is at stake. Following the precedent of the Wilson administration in World War I, the Roosevelt regime had the Federal Bureau of Investigation (FBI) arrest a great many persons with outspoken political sympathies for the far left – communism – and the far right – fascism. Not only suspicious as possible spies, these persons' failure to condone the justness of the American crusade for liberal democracy left them exposed as subversive to the common war effort. The abrogation of civil liberties meant legal persecution of religious dissenters, pacifists, and conscientious objectors like Jehovah's Witnesses and of the reactionary and radical press. "Dr. New Deal" indeed gave way to "Dr. Win-the-War."

To save the world for democracy, the Chief Executive, Franklin Roosevelt – or indeed any individual who might have occupied the wartime Presidency – had to forge a consensus government, a view shared by the rank and file of his own Democratic Party and that of the loyal opposition, the Republicans. Wendell Willkie had no qualms about opposing the Axis powers during the Presidential campaign of 1940, nor did the Republican candidate in 1944, Governor Thomas E. Dewey of New York. By the same token, bipartisan internationalism replaced isolationism in the national legislature, Congress. Small wonder, then, that the third branch of government, the judiciary, fell into line. At the top, the Supreme Court quietly acquiesced to compromising rights normally guaranteed by the Constitution. For example, such a great liberal as Justice Felix Frankfurter – a founder of the American Civil Liberties Union (which opposed the Nisei relocation) – preferred to let Congress change the law rather than have the Court revise the law on its own by interfering with the democratic process. In contrast, Justice Hugo Black dissented in majority decisions which violated guaranteed constitutional liberties. Late in the war, influenced in part by the farcical 1944 "Great Sedition Trial" of several dissenters in a district court, the Supreme Court began to mellow. It reversed earlier convictions of Jehovah's Witnesses and certain political extremists and declared unconstitutional the internment of the Nisei.

The situation of the American Negro community could not be excused as a matter of national security, for the blacks had represented a major segment of the American population since the founding of the Republic. Freed from political slavery eight decades before World War II, they were not alien enemies. Quite simply, they entered the war as economic and social inferiors to the white majority. Racial stereotyping, poverty, inadequate education, marginal health, and Jim Crow segregation in civil and military life continued to plague the blacks, who remained geographically concentrated in the rural South and the ghettos of the urban North. Generally excluded from the American democratic mainstream, the blacks found that the war raised possibilities for them to improve their lot by rallying to the common effort. As the National Association for the Advancement of Colored Peoples (NAACP) argued in its journal, "A Jim Crow army cannot fight for a free world." One prominent black leader in New York's Harlem district, A. Philip Randolph, head of the Brotherhood of Sleeping Car Porters, in mid-1941 threatened

AMERICA AT WAR

a march by 100,000 Negroes from New York to Washington to demand equal employment in the strictly-white defense industries. FDR, strongly advised by New York's Mayor Fiorello LaGuardia, quickly conceded and issued an executive order forbidding racial discrimination in defense factories. He also created the Fair Employment Practices Commission (FEPC) as watchdog, but gave it no regulatory teeth.

The status of the American black during World War II was still fixed by a separate-but-equal interpretation of the Constitution set by the high court as far back as 1896. The equality had never been more than perfunctory in segregated America, but since segregating a war plant was obviously impossible, the Negroes became more outspoken in their demands to be given equal training, jobs, and pay instead of simply menial and unskilled tasks. The same was true over the matter of military service. Although 100,000 black soldiers had enlisted in the Army by the time of Pearl Harbor, and many more followed voluntarily or via the draft, they were generally placed in support rather than combat units – in short, doing the dirty work. And since most Army training camps were located in the South for its year-round warmer climate, racial incidents flared up between white and black trainees on and off the bases. One Negro soldier was even astounded to be turned away from a restaurant in Kansas as German prisoners of war were being served. At least the Army's air force trained an all-Negro fighter squadron, the 99th, though it required a specially-trained all-black ground crew of mechanics. The Navy was at first even more rigid, employing its black sailors primarily as cooks and ammunition passers until it found that they could shoot down just as many planes as whites at their 20mm gun battle stations. In 1943 the Navy joined the Army in commissioning its first Negro officers. The final absurdity occurred during the North African landings in 1942 when black troops were given their own target – landing unopposed in Liberia to build an airfield!

Racial and ethnic prejudice was directed against Italian-Americans, Mexican-Americans, Slavic and Chinese communities, Jews, and others, but the Negro always remained the primary target. As the wartime mobilization caused migrations of persons of all races to the cities seeking jobs in defense plants, daily contacts became inevitable. The result was two-fold: violent clashes over mutual grievances, real or imagined, and the education of whites about the plight of non-white races. Race riots erupted in many cities, the bloodiest being in June 1943 in Los Angeles, where white soldiers and sailors beat up youthful Hispanic "pachuco" gang members, and in Detroit, where blacks and whites fought with a fury that produced 35 fatalities and more than 700 injuries. Lynchings, as in prewar days, continued in the South, and beatings knew no regional focus. But incidents of open white sympathy for blacks also increased at an uncommon pace, especially as blacks began quiet sit-ins at all-white restaurants and in front seats of segregated buses. The First Lady, Eleanor Roosevelt, was particularly active in helping the Negro. Public statements of concern from sensitive leaders like Under Secretary of War Robert Patterson appeared hollow to the frustrated victims of discrimination, but these appeals added to the endless flood of news stories which awakened white America to this blatant contradiction of its moral principles.

The war, in short, provided a catalyst for social change in race relations – not revolutionary by comparison with postwar developments, but certainly dramatic enough to regard the wartime period as a major turning point. Gunnar Myrdal's *An American Dilemma* (1944) was only one of several popular books – fiction as well as nonfiction – to highlight the problem. Gradual integration of public, government, and private establishments, particularly in the North and Midwest, began to increase, especially after FDR strengthened the powers of the FEPC. Many, though not all, labor unions accepted Negro workers, and the military increased its enlistments of blacks, whose growing effectiveness in combat impressed their white comrades-in-arms. In entertainment and the arts, the image of the blacks improved significantly. But, most of all, it was the determination of the blacks themselves which got them and kept them in better jobs and to organize for collective action. The NAACP's membership swelled from 50,000 to 500,000 over the war years. Leaders like A. Philip Randolph and the white A.J. Muste of the Fellowship of Reconciliation urged active though nonviolent protest as preached by India's Mohandas Gandhi. From this strategy emerged the Committee of Racial Equality (CORE), whose patient sit-ins often got results.

America's war, by its very aim of promoting democracy as the global substitute for authoritarian rule, subtly but inexorably forced internal social, economic, and political changes on its own society. The simple, oft-quoted statement of a Negro tenant farmer to his landlord the day after Pearl Harbor bespoke the poignancy of the challenge: "Ah hear dem Japanese gone done dee-clare war on yo' white folks. That right?" In so many ways it was. For Japan had consciously gone to war to expel the Western white colonial powers from Asia. Their own brutal subjugation of other Oriental peoples compromised their appeal as liberators, however, just as the Nazi legions repressed the natives of the countries they overran, including the Russian people tired of communist rule. But just as FDR's vision of the postwar international system was ill-formed and incomplete, so too did he resist instituting direct social changes at home – like abolishing all-white primary elections in the South, lest he alienate the powerful Democratic leadership there. But the days of the old established assumptions of main street America as portrayed in, say, the *Saturday Evening Post*, were markedly shortened by the war.

Economically, the most entrenched element was big business. The tycoons of Wall Street, Chicago, and Detroit had been brought into government to mobilize and manage industry during World War I and had succeeded admirably. After the Armistice, however, their return to prewar classical fiscal practices had proved disastrous, and contributed to the Great Depression. Franklin Roosevelt had courted the giants of the business world in the initial stage of his New Deal and had abandoned notions of balanced budgets in favor of deficit spending – the remedy suggested by British economist John Maynard Keynes. This meant keeping money in circulation by massive government spending but at the cost of driving up the national debt. This approach had not solved all the problems of the Depression, but it had stimulated economic activity. And it had been overseen from the White House – or rather by FDR's "brains trust" of young economic experimenters.

The challenges of World War II mobilization required sound fiscal management of the highest order. For this, the administration had no choice but to turn to the experts from big banking and big business. Some were brought into the existing executive structure – like Forrestal in the Navy, Patterson the War Department, and Robert M. Lovett to mobilize the strategic bomber program in war. Others left the big corporations to become "dollar-a-year" men, heading up the many newly-created wartime agencies for the duration – notably Knudsen of the Office of Production Management and Donald Nelson of the War Production Board. Finally, the industrial giants had to become partners of government in order to deliver the industrial goods. Auto maker Henry Ford typified the traditional industries, while men like Henry J. Kaiser elected to switch from peacetime pursuits to war products – in his case from construction of highways, bridges, and dams to that of ships. And because small businesses had always dominated the economy, Roosevelt and Morgenthau of the Treasury hoped to give them a share of the boom. Governmental interference frustrated many corporate leaders, especially those in the burgeoning aircraft industry; Reuben Fleet of Consolidated Aircraft decided to leave his industry altogether at the end of 1941 because of it.

Charged with creating the greatest war machine in the history of the world, let alone of any democracy, these men wielded immense economic power in the march toward victory. It could have been no other way. Modern, total war with machine weapons and fully-mobilized populations could not be conducted by amateurs. Expert management was the *sine qua non* of new-age superpowers, so much so – though few realized it during the course of the war – that such a military-industrial complex would have to be made permanent in the balance of the postwar superpowers. FDR, having championed social reform in the later period of the New Deal, was determined to maintain as much control as prudent over the mushrooming of wartime business and preserve hard-won

social gains as well as a healthy economy. He had no game-plan but relied on Secretary Morgenthau and a raft of wartime agency heads to police the economy. Whatever he did, he could not tarry. Action became the order of the day, and whenever one program failed, another was tried without delay. As on the New Deal, Roosevelt was an experimenter and power broker who never surrendered leadership of any sector to a subordinate "czar."

To finance the war, therefore, the administration had several options: price controls, increased taxes, deficit spending, and war bonds. From annual prewar federal budgets of under $10 billion, the government would spend a total of $389 billion between mid-1940 and mid-1946, making the task of acquiring adequate revenues a very considerable one. And it had to be done without hurting the average consumer or creating runaway inflation that would inhibit the reconversion to a stable postwar peacetime economy. In July 1940, when France fell, an aroused Congress opted for deficit spending with a new revenue act and by raising the ceiling of the national debt. Furthermore, it authorized the sale of defense bonds and began tinkering with income taxes by slashing exemptions 25 percent. Between the President and Congress, these measures were enhanced and revised as the war went on.

While industrial output blossomed during 1940-41, wages increased, prices rose, and the economy began to inflate. The consumer could now buy more goods, but on the other hand the availability of certain valuable commodities like rubber, aluminum, and sugar had to be restricted from private citizens in favor of war production. All these requirements needed to be coordinated under a centralized agency, which the President established in April 1941 – the Office of Price Administration and Civilian Supply, soon shortened simply to the OPA. For its head he appointed Leon Henderson, a veteran New Dealer long devoted to protecting the consumer. Battling the prosperous auto industry to cut civilian car production in favor of tanks and airplane engines, Henderson won a partial victory in August by convincing FDR to increase his powers. Following Pearl Harbor, Congress empowered the OPA to fix price ceilings on nearly every commodity save farm products (the work of the vocal farm lobby), to ration automobile tires and gas, and to impose rent controls in some 500 areas being glutted by defense workers. Such measures alienated business leaders and consumers alike, especially as inflation and the cost of living rose, but Congress was forced again to broaden the OPA's powers. Finally, FDR created a new Office of Economic Stabilization (OES) late in 1942 to head off rampant inflation. James F. Byrnes stepped down from the Supreme Court to head the new agency, and an unpopular Henderson left the OPA, eventually being replaced by advertising executive Chester Bowles.

Before Pearl Harbor, precious raw minerals were sought from the consumer though scrap drives, especially for aluminum, tin, and rubber – all makeshift efforts which had mixed results. After the country's official entry into the war, the OPA was able to systematize prices and rationing – administered at the local level by volunteer-run War Price and Rationing Boards. The process became exceedingly complex, although patriotic consumers generally complied and even reported violations by shopowners. Many people, however, hoarded rationed goods and created a very profitable and illegal "black market." By the end of the war, no fewer than 8,000,000 items would have price ceiling affixed to them.

Beginning the last week in April 1942, ration books of coupon stamps were issued to each family by the local board – which, incidentally, could favor personal friends. Each adult was allowed a monthly quota of the number of goods he or she could purchase. The consumer was issued a booklet with a six-month supply of ration stamps, each stamp having a "point value" based mostly upon availability of the product. For example, red stamps were used to purchase meat and butter, blue for processed foods. As supplies fluctuated, so did the point value, so that the number of required stamps for each purchase varied from month to month. The actual prices for each item did not usually vary, having been fixed by the OPA. And the buyer was not allowed to hoard stamps from one month to the next. Car owners were issued a booklet with stamps each worth a certain amount – a 2.5, 3 or 5 gallon purchase, but a person

had to display on the windshield a letter designating the weekly gas allowance for that particular car: "A" for general use, "B" for commuting to work, "C" for utilization at work, and "E" for emergency vehicles like police cars, tow trucks, and those used by ministers, and reporters. The consumer kept up with the changing ration quotas through regular announcements by the OPA in the local newspaper.

In the frenzied search for raw materials with which to arm and feed the war machine, the OPA prevailed upon the average citizen to make cuts in daily consumption. Civilian automobile production simply stopped in 1942, and car owners and dealerships learned to stretch the lifetime of the average car up to and beyond 200,000 miles. With gas rationing, a family could not travel very far anyway; the wartime "Victory" speed limit was set at 35 miles per hour, saving wear on autos; the OPA admonished on posters, "Is this trip necessary?" Scrap rubber drives yielded little, but a new synthetic rubber industry made up for the Southeast Asian rubber sources lost to Japan. Extra cooking pots and household tools, as well as accumulated fat and grease from cooking, were collected, although their actual recycling value into planes and tanks was often nil. Similarly, the clothing industry was exhorted to sacrifice high fashion in the interest of saving textiles for uniforms – women's hemlines moved up, men's trouser cuffs came off, shoe styles became bland, and baggy zootsuits of the "hip" set were forbidden. Measuring the actual results of such sacrifices proved elusive. In spite of war profiteers and hoarders, however, most Americans reacted selflessly and patriotically to meet the government's needs.

What hurt most was the rationing of agricultural products as the long arm of the OPA gradually brought these too under control. The major irritant became the cutback on meat availability in March 1943 – each person held to 28 ounces a week, with a similar reduction in the sale of hard cheeses. A meat-eating American had therefore used inflated wartime earnings to enjoy the steak, beef, and chops long absent over the hard Depression decade. Now, however, with cutbacks, whenever the OPA proclaimed a "meatless Friday" the enterprising housewife rose to the occasion by concocting fish, egg, and meatless "meat" dishes like creamed chipped beef gravy on toast – the notorious "S.O.S." in the military. Butter, never abundant because of huge Army and Navy buy-ups of it, fortunately had a substitute for the civilian – oleo-margarine. Made from vegetable oil, it had a taste closely resembling butter, but a pale and unpalatable white color. To overcome this handicap, housewives were taught to kneed a pill-size globule of yellow food coloring into each cake of margarine. This butter substitute worked so well that margarine became a permanent fixture of American eating habits. Other substitutes clearly failed however – imitation chocolate, sweeteners, and soap.

Long lines of buyers became commonplace on the domestic scene not because Americans were starving or lacked the necessities of life – as in Europe and Asia – but because their pockets were full. The defense industry had virtually wiped out unemployment, wages rose as war contracts increased the demand for workers, and with rationing and lack of mobility there was little else for the average American to spend money on. The supplies were there, generally speaking, and more people than ever could afford to buy them.

The wartime cost of living rose nine percent and prices 20 percent above prewar levels during 1941-42, but real earnings for the average workers stayed ahead at 30 percent. By 1943-44 wages had doubled over 1939, as an unskilled worker brought home between $45 and $50 a week, and a skilled one $80 plus fringe benefits like a Christmas bonus. Prices reached their peak by 1943, and OPA director Bowles thereafter managed the impressive feat of holding rises in the cost of living under one-and-a-half percent. The United States became a genuine middle class society as upward economic mobility reduced the ranks of the poor, the wealthy sector diminishing concurrently. The wartime economy meant prosperity for the vast majority of people for the first time in the country's history.

Increased earnings naturally broadened the tax base by which the government could obtain revenues for prosecuting the war. And none could argue with the slogan, "Pay your taxes, Beat the Axis." Furthermore, the tax base was broadened significantly from expanding industries and

AMERICA AT WAR

the huge army of wartime workers – 30 million individual taxpayers in 1942, a sixfold increase in three years. For industry, FDR and Congress had agreed on an excess profits tax in late 1940 by which profits and plant amortizations were adjusted to prevent penalties to corporations and to stimulate mobilization. After Pearl Harbor the new War Production Board (WPB) supported – and the administration and Congress had to agree upon – the setting of excess profits to be taxed at 90 percent, but which with exemptions was really 80 percent – plus an additional guaranteed 10 percent postwar refund. Federal revenue increased, but so did that of big business, which paid higher wages, which were also taxed.

Neither the taxpayer nor his elected representatives in Congress wanted income taxes raised, given the new prosperity. At the practical level, young new wage earners were unaccustomed to saving enough money to pay their annual taxes at year's end. More important, take-home pay was causing inflation to rise, leading the Treasury Department to recommend in 1943 that each worker be taxed as he earned – by withholding part of each paycheck. If adopted, however, taxpayers would be hit doubly, by having to pay their 1942 taxes in the usual lump sum even while having their 1943 taxes withheld. Following the advice of economist Beardsley Ruml, Congress compromised by excusing three-fourths of everyone's 1942 taxes and by not initiatng tax withholding until July 1943. This scheme pleased all taxpayers, but especially those whose enormous 1942 profits would hardly be touched. The government lost important revenue by the arrangement, of course, but 1943 earnings were so high that the loss was not great enough to affect the war effort. And withheld income tax became a permanent feature of American life.

FDR and Henry Morgenthau faced a political crisis over taxes, however, for early in 1942 they wanted to obtain most of their tax revenues from the rich – estate, gift, excise, and luxury taxes – rather than from the lower income groups. Congressional leaders, viewing this as a New Deal anti-business measure for social reform – namely postwar social security services – argued for a general sales tax, which was also supported by liberals Henry Wallace and Leon Henderson, even though it would shift the tax burden to lower-income workers. The resulting revenue bill in October avoided the sales tax but slapped a five percent "Victory tax" on all annual incomes over $624 – an additional burden especially on factory workers – while lowering taxes on the $6,000 to $12,000 income group. War costs soon demanded increased revenues, but Congress early in 1944 passed another pro-business tax bill and overrode the President's veto by a wide margin. The wartime boom which favored the corporations and the growing middle class was not only winning the war but restoring the American economy. Social reform and the New Deal of necessity had to take a back seat to burgeoning wartime prosperity.

But even if income taxes and price controls did not raise all the funds required to achieve victory, the difference was made up by interest-bearing war bonds. Authorized by Congress in mid- 1940, the bonds became Secretary Morgenthau's answer to curbing inflation while raising revenue rather than imposing mandatory savings on newly-prosperous defense workers (which Henderson and Wallace advocated). By being voluntary, Morgenthau reasoned, the bonds would symbolize the individual's personal involvement in America's defense. When the first "Defense Savings Bonds" went on the market in May 1941 he told a national radio audience that purchase of them would "give every one of you a chance to have a financial stake in American democracy." And, he added, they would provide a sound personal investment for any postwar economic turndown (as after World War I) – a rare allusion by any government leader to long-term planning.

With Roosevelt's tacit approval, the Secretary aimed his appeal for bonds – which took the label "war bonds" after Pearl Harbor – at the broad-based market of middle class Americans. As in his desire to open defense plants in the greater Midwest and thus distribute the profits enjoyed in the established factories along the coasts, Morgenthau sought to broaden the base of prosperous Americans where the New Deal had frankly failed. He solicited the advertising industry to sharpen

the appeal, which meant calling upon Americans' hatred of the enemy as much as on the loftier goals of sound investments.

The theme of "sacrifice" by civilians evoked a powerful and positive response from a public aroused and vengeful over mounting casualties among the combat forces. "Minute Men" hawked the bonds along every Main Street in the land. "War loan" drives – seven in all, plus one "Victory loan" drive – leaned heavily upon the entertainment industry to reach middle America. Radio, movie shorts and salesmen in the theaters, and personal appearances by stars from both of the entertainment media achieved huge success. Singer Kate Smith, whose recording of Irving Berlin's "God Bless America" became a veritable anthem for the war years, raised almost $40 million in just one 16-hour radio marathon in mid-1943. The same year a troupe of major Hollywood stars led by James Cagney made a whirlwind tour of 16 cities in three weeks, its highlight being the biggest bond rally of the war – at the foot of the Washington Monument in the nation's capital. Like all Hollywood bond drives, this one exceeded the goal assigned it by the Treasury Department – more than double the $500 million asked for! A special poignancy underscored the meaning of sacrifice on the home front, when, during an early drive, popular actress Carole Lombard (Mrs. Clark Gable) perished in a plane crash.

Between taxes and war bonds, the bulk of the $389 billion war effort was successfully financed. Individuals and corporations paid income taxes that provided nearly $156 billion that were obtained in federal taxes. Of the estimated monies individuals had left after taxes and living expenses, the government figured it gleaned 40 percent in the sale of war bonds – a total figure of another $157 billion. To supplement these vital revenues, the government also borrowed heavily from banks to provide the balance of $76 billion more. The downside of borrowing was that the gross national debt skyrocketed from $34 billion in 1940 to $269 billion six years later. But this was Keynesian economics in its most dramatic role: money stayed in circulation to maintain a healthy, vibrant wartime economy.

Capitalism, the economic component of political democracy, has always been put to its severest test during times of war, when centralized control has been mandatory in the overriding need to fight and achieve victory. The inherent danger, of which Franklin Roosevelt was acutely aware, was that the dollar-a-year men whom he borrowed from industry to direct the economy not be allowed to exceed their powers and thereby weaken the status of the middle and lower socio-economic classes. His prewar New Deal measures had been alternately aimed at restoring upper class business and improving the lot of everyone else. This dual concern had been the essence of American middle class liberalism since the beginning of the republic, but had been pressed most vigorously earlier in the 20th century by the so-called progressive Presidential administrations of Theodore Roosevelt and Woodrow Wilson. The former had been a Republican, the latter, like FDR, a Democrat, meaning that, to Europeans, both American parties were virtually identical – a suspicion confirmed by the apparent similarities between the politics of FDR and his Republican opponents Willkie and Dewey. There simply was no truly conservative element in the American political-economic spectrum to compare with the monarchs, dictators, and aristocrats of Europe who flatly opposed enhancing the social welfare of the lower classes.

Within the context of the American liberal system, however, an economic wedge had been growing ever since the industrialization of the American economy in the late 19th century – the titans of Wall Street who owned the factories versus the blatantly exploited workers in those plants who had been organizing labor unions for collective action to improve their lot. Though championed in theory by progressive politicians of both political parties, the unions had taken direct initiatives to become the outspoken voice of the lower class fighting to participate in the gains of the middle class. These fights had been most violent during the Depression years when factory owners had used force to try to break union-inspired workers' strikes for better wages and safer working conditions. War or no war, organized labor now had no intention of surrendering its hard-earned prerogatives – bargaining collectively and

calling strikes – to the business leaders who now directed wartime industry on behalf of the government.

Throughout the war, FDR tried mightily to balance the two factions. He avoided appointing economic czars on the one hand and on the other tried to blunt union-directed strikes which caused stoppages in war production. The big business faction became the conservative side of the wartime military-industrial combination: corporation executives and Army and Navy officers in charge of military logistical supply. The liberal side followed holdover New Deal social reformers and the powerful leaders of the American Federation of Labor (AF of L), Congress of Industrial Organizations (CIO), and fiercely independent United Mine Workers (UMW). Roosevelt at every turn – by sheer force of his personality if nothing else – tried to check any leader on either side who appeared determined to wield excessive power in wartime America. The economic boom of 1940-41 and the concurrent gains of the growing middle class tended to shift the majority of American public opinion away from the left to the right – as dramatically expressed in the Congressional elections of 1942. And master politician Franklin Roosevelt swung in the same direction – reluctantly – at the expense of his prewar New Deal dreams of social reform and change.

The men of big business – contrary to the claim of prewar pundits that they had caused World War I – did not relish wartime economics, which meant centralized governmental controls, standardization of products, price fixing, and drastically reduced competition. After a decade-long Depression, they were in no mood for regulation, but, if it had to be, at least they wanted to make it work by self-policing. The War Production Board (WPB), instituted in January 1942, was the closest thing to minding their own shop, for its head, Donald M. Nelson, had been executive vice president in charge of purchasing for the vast Sears, Roebuck and Company and then procurement boss of the short-lived Office of Production Management. With the WPB he enjoyed full reign in coordinating the nation's defense industries, although he had to work in close liaison with the OPA in setting prices and rationing quotas, and all actual priorities were set and all contracting done by the Army-Navy Munitions Board, headed by a sharp former Wall street broker, Ferdinand Eberstadt. The latter agency represented the Army and Navy, which resented being subordinated to a civilian agency and head. Thus Nelson and the armed services constantly remained at loggerheads over priorities and allocations of strategic raw materials.

Both the WPB and the military faced a common obstacle in the watchdog Senate Special Committee to Investigate the National Defense Program, chaired by Senator Harry S. Truman. Established in March 1941 after Congressmen learned of waste and profiteering in defense contracts, the Truman committee had been given little encouragement or funding by a skeptical Congress. But the feisty, determined senator from Missouri had been underestimated. He coolly probed into all new defense programs, looking for abuses and inefficiency before any scandals or production losses could develop, then letting other agencies of government take corrective action. His committee's findings on the ineptness of the OPM, for example, were a key factor in the dissolution of this agency in favor of the WPB. As the war progressed, the ubiquitous committee even looked into the activities of organized labor vis-a-vis the war effort. Truman subsequently uncovered and exposed much corruption and mismanagement, thus contributing significantly to the war effort. Not without reason did his reputation as a fair, patriotic investigator make him attractive to the Democratic Party leadership for the Vice-Presidential nomination in 1944.

Notwithstanding the diverse interests of the above agencies, Donald Nelson issued a forthright statement of WPB policy immediately on taking over in January 1942. To insure the 100 percent conversion of the economy to war production, he said he was bringing in all dollar-a-year men from big business to run the several divisions of the Board, against the wishes of the unions and the Truman committee which wanted labor and government to share in the WPB's leadership. The Victory Program for 1942 centered on the need for 45,000 Army tanks, 60,000 Army and Navy aircraft, and 8 million tons of merchant shipping. Ideally, the many small companies of the nation should share in the enterprise, but the urgency of military needs meant that the big ones – experienced and easily adaptable for conversion and expansion – had to be given the major contracts. Thus, the 100 companies producing only 30 percent of the weaponry when the buildup had begun in mid-1940 would be handling over 70 percent by the middle of the war. Nelson himself, like FDR and Morgenthau, wanted to redistribute more of the growing wealth to smaller companies, but the generals, admirals, and Ferdinand Eberstadt insisted, correctly, that efficiency lay in concentrating on the big corporations.

This policy certainly pertained to the production of tanks, planes, and ships. The Detroit auto makers – as always dominated by Henry Ford – easily shifted from cars to tanks and even added airplane engines to their output. General Motors under Charles E. Wilson did the same, eventually opening new plants to turn out Navy planes of designs already under maximum production by Grumman and Chance-Vought. The aircraft industry mushroomed under existing giants like Grumman, the United Aircraft supercorporation in Connecticut (Vought, Sikorsky, Pratt & Whitney engines, and Hamilton-Standard Propeller), Boeing, Martin, and the complex of plants in Southern California – Convair, Douglas, Lockheed, and North American. As for shipping, Henry J. Kaiser emerged as the ultimate giant; his techniques of mass production became so remarkable that he could turn out a Liberty cargo ship in less than a month, not to mention some 50 escort aircraft carriers and other warships to offset shipping losses to the Axis. Small businessmen, New Dealers, the unions, and even FDR and Nelson might complain about so much economic power vested in so few titans of industry, but none could deny the plain fact that they delivered the goods, and in the time required.

During the first half of 1942, in spite of considerable in-fighting and inevitable problems of organizing the WPB, it worked rather well. Then the shortages in rubber and gasoline, which brought on the rationing of both, began to undermine Nelson's leadership. He convinced the President to transfer Eberstadt and the Munitions Board to his own jurisdiction, whereupon the brilliant Eberstadt created the Controlled Materials Plan which greatly streamlined the allocation of strategic materials to the various military programs. Still, the WPB was not working smoothly enough to suit FDR, who thereupon appointed Jimmy Byrnes as Director of Economic Stabilization in November, a new post one notch above Nelson's WPB. The Army, moreover, tried to win direct control over actual production of weapons after the strategic materials had been allocated by the WPB, thereby seeking to erode Nelson's power. Nelson countered by having FDR appoint Charles E. Wilson of General Electric (not to be confused with the "Engine Charlie" Wilson of General Motors) to handle that task within the WPB. Early in 1943 Nelson enlarged Wilson's duties, thus slighting the pro-Army Eberstadt's influence, whereupon the army – and Byrnes – tried to get Nelson fired. Instead, Nelson moved first and sacked Eberstadt.

The dispute struck to the core of American democracy, for Nelson represented the hallowed dictum of civilian control over the military and was accordingly praised by the Truman committee for his stand. Nelson and WPB went about their considerable business with improved controls to achieve the absolute peak of wartime production in virtually all categories during 1943, although Nelson had earned the undying enmity of the Army. As that year drew to a close, Nelson and others could see the first light toward the end of the tunnel of victory – the Allies had begun the offensive on virtually all fronts and would have more than enough men and materials with which to accomplish the task. The idea therefore emerged of reconverting some industries to domestic civilian needs. The military reacted almost hysterically, fearful lest the public stray into a false sense of well-being and slacken its singlemindedness of winning what still promised to be a long war. FDR sided with the military early in 1944 by threatening to call for a national mobilization – a draft of all able-bodied civilians into the wartime labor force.

Thus, new battle lines were drawn between civilian and military agencies over short-term and long-term planning. Roosevelt, with his usual aplomb, mediated by upgrading Byrnes' post of directing economic

AMERICA AT WAR

stabilization to that of heading a new Office of War Mobilization and Reconversion, making Byrnes a virtual "assistant President." Byrnes then enlisted the services of the eminent elder statesman Barnard Baruch, who had headed production during World War I, to recommend a reconversion policy to a peacetime economy. When Byrnes made positive recommendations, based on Baruch's advice, Nelson was charged with the task of initiating the first cutbacks in wartime production. The Truman committee supported it, and Congress passed legislation enabling the disposal of war surplus. But the War and Navy departments counterattacked by promoting a cleavage between Nelson and Wilson within the WPB. The result, complicated but certain, was victory for the military, for Nelson was sent to China to assist in its war production and replaced as head of the WPB by Julius A. Krug in mid-1944. Krug could do little more than give virtual lip service to reconversion and follow the military course of unfettered munitions production.

Nelson, however, had accomplished the job, and the military got what it wanted too – even keeping wartime production in high gear well into 1945 because of German and Japanese counterattacks at the turn of the new year. Like industry, the Navy and the Army Air Forces had no intention of being reduced to inadequate Depression-era levels of strength in the postwar period; they contracted for far more fleet carriers and strategic bombers than could possibly be ready to see action before the end of the war. So Nelson's WPB had mobilized all the steel, copper, coal, and synthetic rubber required to deliver 14 million tons of ammunition, 12 million rifles and machine guns, three-and-a-half million military vehicles, including tanks, nearly 300,000 aircraft, 1,200 warships, over 64,500 assault craft, and more than 5,500 merchant vessels totalling almost 57 million deadweight tons. Far outproducing the enemy, American industrial capacity was able also to furnish much of the necessary military hardware for Great Britain, the Soviet Union, and Nationalist China. Donald Nelson indeed fulfilled Roosevelt's promise to turn the nation into the arsenal of democracy.

Nelson's path – and that of industrial management in general – was plagued throughout the war by organized labor. Although the AF of L of skilled workers, CIO of unskilled, the UMW of miners, and other unions battled each other, they were united in a common effort to protect the gains made for the worker in wages and safe working conditions during the later New Deal. And the ranks of the unions swelled dramatically from 9 to almost 15 million members during the war years. In addition to labor's natural adversaries of industrial management and the military, the general public regarded union agitation and strikes as downright unpatriotic – the same view it held, of course, regarding war profiteers. But the working man wanted to win the war and achieve his fair share in the process.

Two figures dominated the union scene – John L. Lewis and Sidney Hillman. The rambunctious, charismatic Lewis held the reins of both the UMW and CIO at the time when mobilization began in mid-1940. A recent foe of Franklin Roosevelt because the latter had failed to support a strike, Lewis declared he would resign his headship of the CIO if FDR was re-elected in 1940 and then made good on his threat, but he continued to agitate. By contrast, Hillman, founding president of the Amalgamated Clothing Workers of America and first vice president of the CIO, remained a favorite of FDR and believed in working closely with big business to meet the production demands of the war. Roosevelt accordingly appointed him as the laborite co-director of OPM alongside William Knudsen in 1940, in which capacity Hillman tried to persuade more militant union leaders like Lewis to fall into line. Nevertheless, spontaneous wildcat strikes broke out as company profits and inflation soared, whereupon FDR, in March 1941, created the National Defense Mediation Board to settle disputes. Lewis immediately struck with his coal miners and gained a pay hike for them.

The workingman was allowed to keep the 40-hour work week enacted into law in 1938 and additionally to be paid overtime, which the accelerated production schedules demanded, but this did not assuage the discontented as their real buying power declined. More than 3,500 strikes slowed production during 1941 alone, in spite of the efforts of the

Board, whose members included steel organizer Philip Murray, the new president of the CIO. The biggest blowup occurred in June when plant workers of California's North American Aviation struck for a wage increase, which FDR then had crushed by Army troops using tear gas and bayonets. The fact that one of the strike leaders was an avowed Communist provoked widespread anti-union feeling. Then, in November,

Lewis again called a strike of his coal miners, this time to force the creation of a union shop. When the government and business members of the mediation board condemned Lewis, Murray and the other CIO representatives resigned, and the Board collapsed.

A national strike by railroad workers was set for December 7, but the attack on Pearl Harbor that day dashed it. FDR then established the National War Labor Board (NWLB) in January 1942, strengthened by pledges from Murray, Hillman, and the other unions to renounce strikes for the duration. And with the simultaneous creation of Nelson's WPB, FDR appointed Hillman to head its labor division. But the peace lasted only a few months, as organized labor observed that the cost of living had risen 15 percent between January 1941 and May 1942. The NWLB mediated this claim with the smaller steel companies and in July 1942 established the "Little Steel Formula" – allowing raises up to 15 percent. This settled the major problem for the time being, and the AF of L and CIO agreed to cooperate more closely with the government. At that, Lewis broke with Murray and pulled his UMW out of the CIO. To be sure, factory and mine workers were toiling long and hard hours to realize the unprecedented industrial achievement, but they wanted and deserved a share in the huge profits being raked in by their bosses – and walkouts continued unabated, supplemented by blatant worker absenteeism.

John L. Lewis was determined, however, to use his UMW to retaliate against Roosevelt by breaking the Little Steel Formula in favor of increased wages to keep pace with inflation. In April 1943 the mine workers struck again, whereupon the President used his war powers to have Secretary of the Interior Harold Ickes, in his role administering the nation's fuel supplies, seize the mines. And Congress passed the Smith-Connally Act in July, enlarging the President's seizure powers and threatening strike organizers with penalties for work stoppages in defense plants. FDR vetoed it as too threatening, but was overridden by Congress, whereupon Lewis managed to maneuver yet another wage increase, supplanting Little Steel. Then, in December, some railroads

struck, causing FDR to seize all the nation's railroads, although he soon relented, returning them to their owners with a wage adjustment.

The country shared the President's frustration with the unions, which became even more militant when he threatened to draft them *en masse* early in 1944. Then, that April, in a reversal of roles, the chief executive of the Montgomery Ward mail order firm, Sewall Avery, refused to abide by a NWLB ruling over a union contract, whereupon FDR used the authority of the Smith-Connally Act to seize control of the company; soldiers had to carry Avery bodily from his office. After negotiations restored ownership, Avery again defied the NWLB in December, whereupon FDR had the Army seize and operate Montgomery Ward for the duration.

The continuing strikes – nearly 5,000 during 1944 alone – for better worker employment security; the nation's first tentative steps toward reconversion to peacetime, and a growing public nervousness over the possibility of a postwar economic collapse contributed to a grudging national recognition of the legitimacy of labor's genuine needs. The extreme examples of the labor question – Lewis' coal miner walkouts and the Montgomery Ward imbroglio – caused business, labor, and government to begin to close ranks in common cause for more amicable postwar relations. Outside of his UMW, John L. Lewis lost his prominent status as spokesman for the unions to Sidney Hillman, who as chairman of the CIO Political Action Committee actively supported FDR for reelection in 1944. The Smith-Connally Act came to be subtly ignored by all parties, and early in 1945, as strikes were still occurring at a rate of up to 40 per day, labor and business – the U.S. Chamber of Commerce, AF of L, and CIO – finally and formally agreed to cooperate henceforth. Victory in World War II therefore included the ancillary achievement of organized labor's full integration into the mainstream of American political and economic life.

The very foundation upon which the governmental-industrial-labor mobilization rested lay in manpower, that is, the nation's strategic manpower potential. From a total population that passed the 131 million mark in the national census of 1940, the proper and effective distribution of able-bodied adults into the several components for waging total war was crucial: the Army and Navy, the federal bureaucracy, the factories and mines, the farms, and the normal workaday world which had to sustain American society until the great Victory was won. Before Pearl Harbor, mobilization occurred on a fairly haphazard basis, but in April 1942 the administration established the War Manpower Commission to coordinate the effort and maintain the necessary balance between civilian workers and uniformed personnel.

The size of the American adult population proved ideal to meet the nation's needs as long as one realizes that the United States' manpower could not have won the war alone. The vast manpower of the Soviet Union played the key role in defeating the main German armies on the ground in Europe; Britain's and her Commonwealth's manpower acted as virtually full partners of America in the Atlantic and Mediterranean; and China's vast though disparate population was instrumental in tying down the huge major Japanese armies on the mainland of Asia – facts often and unfortunately little understood or appreciated by Americans during or since the war.

America's civilian work force always numbered between 53 and 55 million men and women between 1940 and 1945. Availability of workers fourteen years and older was made possible by employing most of the 9 million men still out of work at the beginning, drawing on teenaged boys and girls as well as retired persons, and – as a last resort – opening up jobs to adult women as many working men entered the armed services. This reluctance may be explained simply by existing social mores of the American family in effect from the earliest days of the American colonies. To cite the fact that 70 percent of British and Russian women served in uniform or factories is a weak comparison, for the immense physical destruction to those countries – and to Germany – simply required that all available persons be mobilized. Britain drafted all workers into its labor force, while the Soviet dictatorship merely intensified its communistic ways of collective production. America's geographic

insularity gave this country an immense advantage – the luxury of having all but 29 percent of its adult women in their usual role of "keeping the home fires burning." Thus, 84 percent of all adult and teenage males "manned" the guns and machines. In addition, using overtime, their average work week climbed over the legal 40 hours to 46.6 during the conflict.

Direct governmental employment eventually absorbed 3,526,000 civilians into the federal system and over 16 million into the military. The fall of France in July 1940 triggered the explosion of jobs, most dramatically when the passage of the Selective Service Act that September tripled the authorized strength of the Army to 1,400,000 – reached the following June. All adult males between the ages of 21 and 35 were obliged to register for the draft on pain of arrest, imprisonment, and a fine for failure to comply. The Selective Service Administration, headed for most of the war by Army General Lewis B. Hershey, established 6,175 local draft boards throughout the land, each generally run by volunteers like the OPA rationing boards. Lots were drawn for numbers assigned to each registered male, who, if he passed his physical and mental examinations, was inducted into the Army for at least eight months of training prior to assignment.

In the century-and-a-half since the adoption of the American Constitution, the need for massive numbers of Army troops had arisen only twice – the Civil War and World War I. In normal peacetime, the first line of defense had always been the Navy, backed up by an array of coastal forts – the dubious effectiveness of which had never been put to the test – and a small frontier army. Now, in 1940-41, still officially peacetime, the nation's third great mobilization of manpower began – with large numbers of volunteer enlistees, activated National Guard units from the states, and a still relatively few draftees. To avoid the draft, or simply due to the lure of adventure, many young men enlisted in the Navy, Marine Corps, or Army Air Corps – none of which required a draft.

Pearl Harbor acted as the catalyst for the Big Expansion. The Army called for another 5 million men and upgraded its Air Corps to be a virtually independent service, the U.S. Army Air Forces (AAF). The draft age was widened with the registration of all men between the ages of 18 and 45, though married men were generally exempted and most over the age of 35 were never called. Draftees began to flood the hastily-erected Army basic training camps at the phenomenal rate of 100,000 a month. The U.S. Coast Guard was transferred from the Treasury Department to the Navy for the duration, and the Navy began drafting young men in December 1942. Despite the dogged resistance of Congressmen fearful that the virtues of American womanhood would be compromised if females were allowed to enlist, they were clearly needed in order to release men from support, clerical, and administrative tasks. Eleanor Roosevelt lent a subtle hand to the advocates, and during 1942 all the services established special branches for them – Women's Army (Auxiliary until 1943) Corps (WACs), Women's Auxiliary Ferrying Squadrons (WAFS), Women Marines (in 1943), and Coast Guard Women's Reserves (SPARs for the Guard's motto and translation for *Semper Paratus*- Always Ready. And the American Women's Volunteer Service – ultimately 260,000 strong – took up auxiliary duties for the military and civilian sectors alike.

By mid-war, 1943, the Army and AAF decided to increase its ranks to 7,700,000 and surpassed that figure to 8,300,000 by the end of the fighting. By then, the Navy numbered 3,400,000 men and women, the Marine Corps over 484,000, and the coast Guard more than 170,000. Women numbered about 350,000 in all. Although the merchant marine was a civilian enterprise, the manpower it required both to build and crew the vessels which supplied the Allied fighting forces around the world was crucial. At peak capacity, the eight government and many more private shipyards employed a total of 800,000 persons, their subcontractors nearly 600,000. To coordinate wartime merchant shipping and training of officers and crews, the President created the War Shipping Administration in February 1942; it undertook the training of more than 315,000 men before the war ended.

During 1940-41 the Navy, led by its vigorous aviation community in

AMERICA AT WAR

the Bureau of Aeronautics, pioneered the acquisition of top talent from the business, legal, banking, and insurance professions by awarding direct commissions for men in their late twenties and thirties. Such innovations recognized the need for skilled managers in this complex war, followed in the Navy by deferred programs for college students in specialized V-1, V-5, V-7, and V-12 programs, resulting in commissions and/or possible flight training as naval aviators. The AAF and Army in general followed suit, stimulating the general revolution in wartime management that would become a permanent feature of the postwar armed services.

The role of women in World War II America, as in so many aspects of national life, was not new. Female clerks and military auxiliaries like the Navy's yeomanettes had been important during the first war. But the sheer scale of the 1940s conflict made women's participation immense and with it an indelible impression that would add so much fuel to the women's liberation movement a generation later that male-female relations would never again be the same. The number of women workers rose from 12 to 18 million between 1940 and 1945 – 5 million of them in industrial plants – from one-fourth to one-third of the nation's entire work force. In the shipyards alone, they comprised an average 17 percent of the total number of laborers. What these figures do not reveal, however, is the fact that women had a high turnover rate in their jobs or were employed only part time because of their desire or need to return to being homemakers.

As poster art propaganda pronounced, the women of America rolled up their sleeves just like the men and took the nickname "Rosie the Riveter" or, as the technology of joining sheet metal changed from rivets to welds, "Winnie the Welder." The special talents of women in precision, meticulous tasks made them downright superior to men in many areas – a boon especially to aircraft manufacturing. By the same token, however, they represented a threat to jobs theretofore monopolized by the men, who generally and not surprisingly resented them. Unfortunately, this bias was shared by plant owners and managers, who paid them lower wages than the men, and by union bosses, who made no excuses for expecting them to give up their jobs as soon as the fighting men returned to reclaim those same jobs. On the other hand, the very presence of the fairer sex required cleaner sanitation facilities, better safety measures, modest child-care centers, and even health and psychological care to meet their special needs and to keep up their morale. "Rosie" responded by doing her patriotic best to become a full partner in the war effort – and with less complaining in spite of considerably more matters to complain about than the men.

As in all of America's wars – large and small – women kept the home fires burning, whether or not they took a job with industry or government. As homemakers, they raised the children by themselves, endured loneliness and worried endlessly about their loved ones overseas, rationed and coped to make ends meet, and volunteered on a huge scale in neighborhoods and communities. They worked in churches, local Red Cross chapters, as civil defense spotters, and as auxiliaries of the American Legion – 2,500,000 members in the latter alone. And when their loved ones did not come back, they suffered untold anguish – the most dramatic example being the deaths aboard the cruiser *Juneau* in 1942 of the five Sullivan brothers, whose sister then enlisted in the waves. But they endured, the bereaved but proud displaying their "Gold Star Mother" flags in the front windows of their homes.

Women and their children also lent a major hand in meeting the agricultural needs of the fighting men of America and the Allies. To fill in for menfolk who left the farms to enter the service, they assumed additional tasks throughout the farm belt of middle America. And in the cities they grew and tended their own "Victory gardens." Whatever they consumed of home-grown vegetables and fruits left more agricultural products to be released for the war effort. Draft boards had little sympathy for keeping farmers at home for food production, a short-sightedness not rectified nationally until mid-1943 when 2 million farmers were deferred from the draft. The year before that, Mexico and the United States agreed to allow Mexican citizens to be employed on American farms, followed by laborers from the British West Indies and Bermuda. Finally, in 1944-45, German and Italian prisoners of war were put to work on the farms, which had the side effect of educating these enemies about the advantages of the American way of life. (No Japanese prisoners were used, since most of Japan's fanatical soldiers preferred death to surrender.)

The proportion of farm to city dwellers in America had been shifting predominantly to the cities ever since World War I, a trend that was accelerated by World War II, during which 5 million people (17 percent of the population) migrated to the cities or entered into the military. No longer in the majority, farmers had evolved into a privileged minority of American economic life, requiring federal subsidies to bring their prices to a rough par – "parity" – with the rest of the country. Unlike industrial workers who unionized to protect their wages, America's 6 million farmers were self-employed and therefore fiercely independent. Collective action was therefore not their style, although among several farm organizations the American Farm Bureau Federation of large farm-owners boasted one million members by the end of the war. The basic unit of agriculture was the family farm, but of the 6 million across the land no less than 96 percent earned annual incomes under $10,000 and employed few if any hired hands. Indeed, net income of the average farm worker was only $738 per annum in 1941, more than doubling to $1,545 in 1945, in contrast to the industrial worker at $1,495 and $2,300 respectively.

Charged with feeding wartime America and much of the world – notably Britain and Russia – American agriculture rose admirably to the challenge. Initial fears that continued peacetime price supports were necessary proved unfounded in the wartime boom, for prices rose and remained consistent with the rest of the economy. Early in 1942 the Department of Agriculture adopted the motto "Food Will Win the War and Write the Peace," meaning that farm production and prosperity would do the job at hand and continue unabated into the postwar period. The farmer made good almost at once, boosting production of the basic commodities – wheat, corn, rice, cotton, peanuts, and tobacco, but also potatoes, eggs, and hogs – so much that American wartime consumers ate more in quantity and quality – resulting in better nutrition and health. The WPB oversaw farm production during 1942, rationing only sugar and coffee. But growing needs led the Agriculture Department to be turned into the War Food Administration in early 1943 in order to initiate the point rationing of meat and selected processed commodities. At the urging of labor to halt rising costs of meat and butter, FDR used Reconstruction Finance Corporation funds to subsidize both products – and added 16 more by war's end.

Total acreage increased by only 5 percent – to 359,000,000 acres – during the war, indicating that improved techniques of food production accounted for the phenomenal boom. Farm mechanization and electrification, already spreading thanks to the New Deal, continued at a far greater pace. In addition to milking machines and combines which harvested and bailed, the number of tractors increased from 1,445,000 to 2,072,000 between 1939 and 1945. Improved fertilizers and the use of the insecticide DDT – discovered a year before Pearl Harbor – stimulated bumper crops, while dehydrated vegetables caused a minor revolution in food processing (although powdered eggs had no popularity among the fighting men). With tin shortages, canning of fruits as well as vegetables had to be replaced by freezing, another vast improvement that would also "write the peace." Similarly, housewives learned to "can" their own vegetables and fruits in jars by learning to use pressure cookers – theretofore the province of commercial canning companies.

Small wonder, then, that total wartime farm income doubled between 1939 and 1943 (with only modest gains thereafter), and overall net income tripled beyond the $5.3 billion level of 1939. Farm prices also doubled, achieving 131 percent of the parity scale based on the base years 1910-14. American agriculture fed the world – victors as well as vanquished – and established its own general stability within the national economy.

Like so much else in wartime America, however, farm prosperity had

its down side for those persons crowded out by the sheer scale of the expansion. In this case it was the small farmer. In steady retreat ever since the rise of large farms at the turn of the century, the poorer tenant farmers and sharecroppers had been rescued by the New Deal – notably by the Farm Security Administration (FSA) and its attendant Farmers Union, representing some 3 million small farmers by the time war struck. The richest farmers, supported by their farm bloc in Congress and the Farm Bureau Federation, used price stabilization to enhance their own prosperity and thereby reduce the competition of the FSA and its clientele. To be sure, both sectors of agriculture shared in full measure the success of wartime farm production, but the high-powered offensive by Big Farming succeeded in reducing the FSA to impotence, thereby assuring the same kind of postwar economic dominance as Big Business and Big Labor.

The principal means of transportation of men, materials, and food across America to the coasts was, as in peacetime, the railroad. In the two weeks following Pearl Harbor, the Army moved 600,000 troops by Pullman cars and coaches to key depots and thereafter claimed priority on all passenger trains for the duration. To regulate the complexities of continental logistics, the Office of Defense Transportation coordinated rail traffic, especially the long freight trains which clogged main and trunk lines and whose box cars had to be carefully distributed among rail sidings until room could be found to remove them to the coasts. Great Lakes ore and grain carriers and river barges supplemented this traffic, as did trucks. But civilian passengers immobilized by gas rationing had to depend on buses and whatever space was available for them on trains. As for the commercial airlines, Donald Nelson, in one of his first acts as head of the OPA, froze airplane seats for military personnel and key businessmen, forcing civilians to take pot-luck and accept the risk of being "bumped" while awaiting plane changes. The rails simply formed the main arteries of the nation's overland traffic, however, and the number of ton-miles of rail increased from 379 billion in 1940 to 747 billion in 1944.

Withal, the United States of America enjoyed immense prosperity during World War II. The gross national product blossomed from around $90 billion to nearly $200 billion, stimulated by a federal budget that increased ten-fold from 1939 to $100 billion at the finish. The median 1940 family income – $1,463 – paled, especially in cities inundated by industries and the attendant services: by 1945 a Los Angeles family earned $3,469, New York $4,044, and Washington, D.C. a whopping $5,316. With extra money to spend, even after taxes and purchases of war bonds, Americans sought ways to spend in the face of rationing, lack of mobility, and want of luxury items. They frolicked and spent extravagantly whenever possible, leading to the most common warning from the more cautious: "Don't you know there's a war on?"

Availability rather than prices determined the market. So a new model 1940 or 1941 motorcar cost $1,200, and used car dealerships and auto mechanics developed ingenious techniques to keep existing cars in operating trim and to recap or retread tires after rationing set in. Gasoline slowly edged toward 20 cents a gallon and motor oil to 25. Meats came to 23 cents per pound for steak, 25 for hamburger, 13 for lamb, and 13 for hot dogs. For an 8-cent loaf of bread, one could spread real butter purchased for under 40 cents a pound. Vegetables were usually available, a 5-cent price tag for a "bunch" of carrots being typical of the low costs. Small-town movie theaters dominated the entertainment scene, day and night, at prices between 25 and 60 cents, and nearly every family had a radio, every other teenager a phonograph for spinning records that cost upwards of 35 cents when they could be had.

As during the depths of the Depression, some 15 million Americans migrated to the new jobs, and every region flourished. Large cities became even larger, tank towns transformed into boom towns. Army camps and Navy stations sprang up in rural areas of the South and Far West. War plants and shipyards expanded on both coasts and appeared anew in the otherwise agrarian Midwest. Shortages in wood and other construction materials did not deter builders from fashioning makeshift dwellings from scraps and abandoned warehouses – and prefabricated

homes offered some respite from the pressure. Established homeowners took in workers needing a rented room, and costs of rented bungalows shot up, forcing many families to live in trailers. Hotels were always full, leading to universal frustration for travelers, embodied in the tune, "I'm Going Mad for a Pad (Are There No Rooms to be Had?)." War Housing Centers tried to control the massive overcrowding, and the National Housing Agency funded the construction of over 1,000 boomtowns accommodating a total of one-and-a-half million people. Even resorts were converted into rest and rehabilitation centers for the wounded brought back from the war fronts. No wonder that congestion and tensions rose, affecting all aspects of community life and leading to riots and ethnic violence from the biggest wartime melting pot of all, Detroit, down to small, formerly sedate towns.

Inevitably, workers who labored strenuously by day – including overtime and the nighttime "swing shifts" – cut loose after hours to relax and to enjoy their earnings. In the cities, posh nightclubs and sleazy flesh traps drew them in, acting as magnets for young Americans liberated from the financial and social strictures of Old Man Depression. Such a new-found freedom combined with the emotional intensity of the war effort to create a virtual round-the-clock party time for off-duty workers and soldiers. In spite of the shortage of real Scotch caused by Hitler's U-boats, and the diversion of alcohol into gunpowder and torpedo manufacture, lesser-quality booze flowed freely. The wartime curfew of 1 a.m. troubled gin mill operators not at all; said New York restaurant owner Toots Shor, "Hell, if you can't get drunk by 1 a.m., you ain't trying." But such excesses also spurred prohibitionist sentiment among reformers – to little avail. Families, however, entertained more at home and put away formal dress for the duration as the war spawned a more informal approach to life.

To counteract the dangerous distractions of homegrown sin centers and latter day camp followers, national and local agencies took action. Most prominent was the USO, United Service Organizations, which offered clean entertainment and hostesses in every city with military installations nearby. The entertainment industry, churches, and communities opened similar "canteens" that provided recreation, theater tickets, dancing, and visits with local families. The loosened morals encouraged many young women to dispense sex so prolifically that they outdid full-time prostitutes. Many were just having fun, while others justified it as helping the troops in time of war, calling themselves "Victory girls." Venereal disease spread so dramatically that former "untouchable" G-man Eliot Ness was appointed national director of Venereal Disease Control. And the military set up "pro stations" to dispense prophylactic services to servicemen. The intensity of the hour led to one-night stands in sleazy hotels but also to innumerable hasty marriages – "for tomorrow we die." Some women even married more than one war-bound soldier boy for his $10,000 insurance policy. Needless to say, a good many wartime unions barely survived. But many did, for the war produced a camaraderie and emotional closeness that forged an entire generation.

Life styles adjusted to wartime shortages as well as innovations. Women's fashions took on a looser look and tailored suits with padded shoulders, along with the just-above-the-knee length hemlines ordered by the OPA. Hair was swept up and covered by bandannas at work for safety, by turbans at play when permanents were not possible, and by a loose net known as a "snood" for shopping. The casualness of the time made slacks a staple too. Silk for stockings went into parachutes, followed in 1942 by the newly-manufactured nylon, which was also withdrawn for military use. A suntan was the summer substitute for such hose, and some determined gals took to having their legs spray-painted and a "stitch" painted down the calf. Men's suits changed little, save for fewer cuffs and the occasional substitution of a bow tie for the usual bib tie. The kids continued to experiment with zoot suits until the OPA cracked down on such wastage of fabric. Everybody's shoes suffered from leather shortages, and people cleansed themselves with soap or soap substitutes to prevent what Lifebuoy soap called "B.O." (body odor).

AMERICA AT WAR

The critical shortage of rubber did not hurt the consumer much beyond the want of automobile tires, for the virgin industry of plastics filled the void for virtually all former rubber products, as well as aluminum, wood, glass, and even cardboard – in pots and pans, fountain pens, thermos bottle covers and especially toys. Cellophane replaced tin foil in chewing gum wrappers. Paper shortages meant that grocery shoppers kept and reused brown paper bags over and over, and lack of Christmas cards in 1943 meant letters instead. That year pennies had to be made from gray steel rather than critical copper, and nickel disappeared from nickel coins. The most mortifying and potentially dangerous shortage turned out to be alarm clocks, the manufacture of which was halted by the OPA in July 1942 to preserve metals. But when workers began to arrive often late for work early in 1943 the WPB had to authorize production of 1.75 million cheap "Victory clocks."

While young marrieds, separated for most of the duration, had to await the postwar period to begin the "baby boom" that would reshape the economy in years to come, the adolescent generation of the war years developed the modern American phenomenon of the teenager. This worthy had already begun to make his/her statement in the immediate prewar years, dancing the frenetic jitterbug while worshipping at the altar of swing bandleaders, most prominently Benny Goodman of the white bands and Duke Ellington of the black. The "kids'" parents liked to dance too, though more sedately to the foxtrot "sweet" bands typified by Guy Lombardo and Sammy Kaye. The change in wartime tastes merged generational popular musical tastes in the orchestra of Glenn Miller, who melded swing and sweet to make him "king of the juke boxes" from 1939 until he joined the Army Air Forces in late 1942. The nickels put into the phonograph juke boxes continued to play his music throughout the war, but the frenzy of good times caused most bands to blow hot and wild during personal and radio appearances. And young boys who grew up in uniform jitterbugged with each other while listening to V-Discs sent overseas to them by the Armed Forces Radio Service.

Teenage girls at home, however, perhaps in reaction to the violence of war and in sympathy with lonesome older siblings, took to pining romantically for attractive male idols. Movie stars like Clark Gable and Errol Flynn attracted their attention, but no man had more appeal to them than the slight, handsome crooner Frank Sinatra. The gals shrieked and swooned at the sound of his voice, their hearts palpitating when they saw him in person. Replete in their bobby sox, they chased him in fantasy if not in person – to the chagrin of parents and teenage boys alike. The Sinatra phenomenon was symptomatic of changing American tastes; the long struggle against Depression and war spelled doom for hot jazz and swing in favor of sentimentality and a quieter peace. The war killed the big bands in other ways too – a musician's union strike which stopped record production over lack of royalties for records played on the radio, a dearth of room on trains for bands accustomed to in-person one-night dances across the country, and the rank commercialization of those bands to suit public tastes. What was more, individual singers were cheaper than full orchestras.

The demise of the big bands also reflected racial influences. The white groups like Goodman's and Miller's did not change their successful musical formulas, while black audiences and musicians looked to innovations, just as Negro culture had originally spawned jazz music as America's one true original art form before World War I. So while black big bands like Lucky Millinder's and Earl Hines' catered to black jitterbuggers in New York's Harlem theaters and dance halls, experimenters Dizzy Gillespie on trumpet and Charlie Parker on saxophone developed the bebop sound in Harlem clubs leading small combos. These also reflected the blacks' frustrations with white music and white tastes and would completely supplant the big bands in the postwar years. As Negro Americans in general continued to seek a unique identity, this modern twist to non-danceable jazz never gained the wide audience that prewar and wartime swing had.

Teenagers at home followed much of this musical activity, widening the gulf with their parents as the kids faced major adjustments at home and in their local schools. The migrations of families, the increased emotional strains of crowded urban living and mixing, and the absence of fathers who had provided stability and discipline all led to a 16 percent rise in juvenile delinquency. The movement of families similarly caused enrollments to drop in many schools, especially in the black South, and to skyrocket in the boom towns. As early as mid-1941, the federal government began to pump money into such afflicted districts, thereby uplifting the quality of education in places like the South, where it had never been strong. The colleges suffered equally, because college-age men were going off to war. So the colleges began to abbreviate degree programs by one year and to solicit the government-sponsored contracts which resulted in the training programs for future officers. The scheme worked, bringing 400,000 men into the colleges, although regular graduating classes were notable by the absence of men. Female coeds spent a lonely tenure in college stripped of regular students of the opposite sex – finalized early in 1944 when the Army pulled out all its uniformed students for reassignment.

The health of the American people reached such unprecedented heights during the war that the life expectancy of whites rose three years, blacks five years, and infant mortality dropped. Part of the reason was more balanced meals from the plentiful supply of vegetables and fruits and the use of vitamins to fortify breakfast cereals and of essential minerals such as iron and riboflavin in flour for bread. Shortages of doctors and dentists became acute as the armed forces put great numbers of them into uniform. Inadequate supplies of medicine led to hoarding, and children's epidemics of measles, mumps, meningitis, and scarlet fever persisted, joined by a disquieting rise in polio cases. But British developments with penicillin in 1941 led to massive production of the medicine in America within three years – successful in curing pneumonia and treating wounds. Sulfa drugs crucial to healing the wounded in battle found an equally ready market at home.

Homemakers learned to "make do" in health care, however, for the first time having sufficient money to spend on it. The military rescued perhaps 2 million men from medical problems by giving them proper attention and diets. Prepaid health insurance plans grew after concerned industrialist Henry J. Kaiser attacked the unsympathetic and profit-conscious American Medical Association in the courts and won on the grounds that the AMA represented an illegal monopoly. The U.S. Public Health Service used federal funds to build and staff hospitals and clinics across the land. Wartime America created the most robust population of any nation in the world.

No greater arena of home front competition between the democratic Allies and totalitarian Axis was more decisive than in mobilized science. Predictably, Hitler assembled his brilliant scientists at government installations under the watchful eyes of the Gestapo, which inhibited unfettered scientific research. The Americans and British, by contrast, allowed their scientists to work in their own universities and private laboratories with general government contracts. In the United States, this sprawling network was coordinated by the Office of Scientific Research and Development (OSRD), created in mid-1941 and headed by Dr. Vannevar Bush. It embraced the 26-year-old National Advisory Committee for Aeronautics and the year-old National Defense Research Committee, both of which had been headed by Bush. The OSRD obtained draft exemptions for nearly 10,000 young scientists and virtually drafted all major research scientists into wartime programs. Bush parceled out contracts to key institutions to meet the needs of the military, most prominently, Woods Hole Oceanographic Institute for underwater devices necessary to defeat Hitler's submarines, the California Institute of Technology to push rocketry and torpedo warfare, and Philadelphia's Franklin Institute to combine Britain's radar with the first crude computers to increase the accuracy of antiaircraft guns and aerial bombing. Many lesser but phenomenal scientific developments emanated from 20 key universities and other laboratories under OSRD direction to give the Allies a critical edge in weaponry over the scientists of Nazi Germany.

The one major exemption to the practice of dispersed scientific research was the development of the atomic bomb. During the preceding decade, astrophysicists had finally discovered that the source of energy

which powered the sun and stars was nuclear reactions. The idea that such a force could actually be reproduced in the laboratory for military uses came to the attention of President Roosevelt in October 1939 when the father of relativity, Albert Einstein, wrote a letter to FDR suggesting that Germany was capable of developing such a nuclear bomb of infinite power. FDR did little more than turn the information over to his scientists,

who, with Bush's support in 1941, worked diligently at the University of Chicago to try to create a chain reaction by splitting the Uranium 235 atom into plutonium. Under the guidance of Italian-born physicist Enrico Fermi, an emigré from fascism, the team achieved success in December 1942. By then, the entire effort was top secret, and many brilliant scientists were recruited to try to create a bomb capable of wreaking immense destruction on the enemy. In May 1943 the Manhattan Project was established under Army control to direct the program using American, British, and Canadian scientists. To obtain the necessary funding without breaching the mandatory secrecy, Bush, Secretary of War Stimson, and Army Chief of Staff General George C. Marshall privately enlisted the support of key Congressional leaders.

The public never knew of the Manhattan Project, although sprawling but closely-guarded research centers at Oak Ridge, Tennessee; Hanford, Washington; and Los Alamos, New Mexico attested to some kind of important war work going on. Under the military authority of Major General Leslie R. Groves and the scientific direction of Dr. J. Robert Oppenheimer, the Project engineers and physicists expended $2 billion at a relentless pace to produce an atomic bomb before the Nazis did. Their Herculean efforts succeeded, and when Germany surrendered in May 1945 the Germans revealed no evidence of ever having even made

the attempt, mainly because of inadequate materials, the press of other war needs, and Hitler's preference for more promising "miracle" weapons like the V-2 inter-range missile. Still, the fear of horrendous human losses in the projected invasion of Japan – and a deepening suspicion over a hostile postwar Soviet Union – led the government to press on in hopes of impressing both these nations. The first atomic blast occurred at a test site at Alamagordo, New Mexico, in mid-July 1945, and two A-bombs were then dropped on the Japanese cities of Hiroshima and Nagasaki three weeks later. The terrible destruction they inflicted helped convince Japan to surrender before the invasion – and Russia was impressed, though not surprised, since its spies had kept the Kremlin informed of the project. So, too, were the American people suitably awed by the achievement.

Aside from the censorship over scientific weaponry, the American people were kept remarkably well-informed about the course of the war by the media – newspapers, radio, and motion picture newsreels. War correspondents and photographers from all the major papers sent back a steady stream of news accounts obtained in the very heat of battle. Many even caught the essence of the real war for the average G.I. Joe – a dirty battle of survival against a cunning, determined foe, with the high-falutin' rhetoric of the flagwavers left behind at home. None caught the intimate side of the dogface's travails better than Ernie Pyle's columns and Bill Mauldin's cartoon characters Willie and Joe in the Italian campaign. Readers could slog ashore with Richard Tregaskis, whose reflections appeared in book form as *Guadalcanal Diary*. And the reporting was sometimes abruptly stilled, as when early in 1944 the respected news analyst Raymond Clapper perished in a midair collision during the carrier raid on Truk lagoon, and a year after that when the beloved Ernie Pyle fell to a sniper's bullet on an islet near Okinawa.

The tightly-edited visual images in Movietone News clips at local theaters carried the magisterial voice of the familiar Lowell Thomas, and the popular March of Time films were narrated by the sonorous intonations of Westbrook Van Voorhis: "Time marches on!" But no medium provided quicker, or more popular news coverage than radio. Americans already accustomed to FDR's Fireside Chats and on-the-spot "remote" broadcasts fine-tuned their radio dials to hear H. V. Kaltenborn, Raymond Gram Swing, William L. Shirer, and Edward R. Murrow report from the war fronts and the news centers directly into their living rooms. American life revolved so completely around radio that a battleship bombardment of the Japanese coast in 1945 was actually scheduled to accommodate a radio timetable. All that the listener had to do was let his imagination create the picture while radio provided the sound – a unique combination which greatly enhanced the emotional drama of the entire era.

Part of radio's subtle message was shared by the advertising industry. Deprived of massive advertising in newspapers and magazines because of paper shortages, the ad men turned to radio and billboards. But also lacking many consumer products to hawk because of the conversion to military output, the hucksters turned the clever trick of identifying commercial firms with those military goods – like "Lucky Strike green has gone to war," the fabrication of the idea that the green wrapper of this cigarette company had been switched to white in order to conserve the chemical used for green coloring. Advertising put forward only a rosy picture to promote the confidence of the average consumer to keep buying their products, a ploy which angered the more sober realists who viewed the war for the violent struggle it was, being fought over major issues. The Coca-Cola Company, for example, produced magnificent color paintings of rosy-cheeked, smiling war workers and troops around the world dutifully interrupting their labors to enjoy a Coke. Indeed, those Coca Cola cheeks even succeeded in creating the standard image of Santa Claus for years to come. The War Advertising Council, however, helped to check inflation and prepared the people for reconversion to peacetime with tantalizing visions of new and revolutionary products for Everyman and Everywoman. Refrigerators and autos would no longer be scarce, but microwave ovens would take decades to reach the average kitchen, and the prospect of ubiquitous home-owned private airplanes alongside cars would turn out to be pure fantasy.

AMERICA AT WAR

Another and more important type of advertising was "selling" the war to the American people – domestic propaganda. Unlike the Wilson administration in World War I, which had had to tightly control and promote America's cause because of less-clear issues, Franklin D. Roosevelt had the catalyst of Pearl Harbor to keep in the mind's eye throughout the duration. This obvious convenience led many cynics and Roosevelt-haters to hypothesize that he had even engineered the sneak Japanese attack as a device for unifying the people. The succession of American and Allied defeats in the eleven months following Pearl Harbor, however, seriously threatened the people's morale – as did the sheer tedium of self-sacrifice and rationing even after the Allies assumed the offensive. Political cartoonists, filmmakers, and advertisers needed no government impetus to caricature the symbols of the evil foe – Adolf Hitler, Benito Mussolini, and Emperor Hirohito or Prime Minister Hideki Tojo. Racial images were especially simple to invoke on the treacherous "Japs" – slanted eyes, yellow skin (of cowards), and buck teeth. The dictators simplified the matter of Americans hating the enemy rather than having to focus on more abstract ideas.

But the problem of sustaining morale was more complex than that, for in a modern total war of entire civilian populations any government needs formal propaganda machines. Indeed, at the time of Hitler's invasion of Poland to start the war in September 1939, the United States was alone among the major powers in having no such agency. Before the year ended, therefore, FDR established the Office of Government Reports, a fairly innocuous body that did little more than keep the people abreast of the national defense program. A series of other similar agencies followed to strengthen the public support of American preparedness, culminating in the Office of Facts and Figures (OFF) in October 1941. Headed by the poet Librarian of Congress Archibald MacLeish, it endeavored to systematize the release of information to the press and people but was never able to satisfy their thirst for detailed information. The attack on Pearl Harbor in December made MacLeish's task even more difficult, given the need for censorship – whereupon FDR on the 19th created the Office of Censorship under newspaperman Byron Price. Both agencies tried to repress journals with a defeatist outlook and worked with the press in preventing the publication of information that might prove useful to the enemy. Price's office survived throughout the war, but the OFF and other agencies involved in domestic propaganda soon proved to be downright inadequate.

In June 1942, the President therefore merged most of these units into one grand superagency – the Office of War Information (OWI) under the highly respected newscaster Elmer Davis. On the one hand, it disseminated propaganda overseas to Allies and Axis alike. On the other, it was tasked with making the often ill- defined goals and programs of the government understandable to the great American public. It was an almost impossible charge, for the scrupulously honest Davis intended to keep the people informed of all pertinent information while being expected simultaneously to act as publicist for administration policies. The Army resented his demands for facts about defeats and casualties as well as victories and his desire to discuss the necessity to begin reconversion, while OPA officials wanted to cover up the confusion over rubber and gasoline rationing, and industry leaders preferred to minimize the news about strikers' grievances. Congress became especially critical of the OWI's publication of insipid propaganda journals and came to regard the agency as a public relations tool of the President and the New Deal; white Southerners also resented its praise of the black contribution to the war effort. The opposition succeeded in cutting the OWI's appropriation so drastically in June 1943 that Davis had to shut down all 46 of its regional offices, thus terminating domestic propaganda altogether. The overseas branch carried on to the final victory, but the Army generally called the tune. Managing information in a democracy at war is always a delicate task, and Elmer Davis accomplished as much as perhaps any person could have in his place.

No-one could dispute the need for and importance of heroes, especially in the early stages of any war before heroism had ceased to be a novelty. Thus B-17 pilot Captain Colin P. Kelly, Jr., was posthumously honored for giving his life to sink the Japanese battleship *Haruna* in Philippine waters just days after Pearl Harbor (though this ship was in fact not sunk until the last month of the war). The doomed defenders of Wake Island became instant martyrs by radioing "Send us more Japs" before being overrun (yet the survivors later revealed they had sent no such message). General Douglas MacArthur, charismatic and newsworthy, became an object of admiration in spite of having to abandon the Philippines (and consciously kept up a public relations campaign till the end of the war). American individualism had for a generation been most visibly revealed in the country's daring airmen, including air racer Jimmy Doolittle and World War I fighter ace Eddie Rickenbacker. So both earned genuine plaudits in 1942 – Colonel Doolittle for leading Army B-25 bombers from the mythical "Shangri-La" (actually the carrier Hornet) in the first bombing of Tokyo, and Eastern Airlines president Rickenbacker for surviving 24 days with others in life rafts in the South Pacific after the B-17 in which he had been a passenger had ditched at sea after losing its compass and radio and running out of gas. Reports of heroism flooded the news media for the duration and did much to sustain Americans' patriotism without government prompting.

Tinsel heroes and newsmakers abounded aplenty as well, stealing headlines from the steady diet of important war news. Suave swashbuckling actor Errol Flynn found his popularity surge from a sensational statutory rape trial over the winter of 1942-43. Verdict: Not guilty. Though many small-town newspapers could not spare the space to carry the trial, the troops overseas got a boot out of it and brought home a new popular phrase, "In Like Flynn." In July 1943 the murder of the British millionaire Sir Harry Oakes in the Bahamas titillated the American reading public before the trial of the prime suspect ended four months later with another not-guilty verdict. Concurrent with the Flynn and Oakes exhibitions and well into 1944 actor Charlie Chaplin faced a paternity suit that was first deflected into a mistrial, then terminated with Chaplin having to pay child support – even though the jury admitted he could not have been the father. The foibles of Americans were no different in war than in peacetime, and the fact that the newspaper readers followed the antics of the upper set did no harm.

The tastes of the average American were pretty simple, meaning that the entertainment industry had to play to those tastes if it was to reap profits from amusement-starved patrons with extra change to spend – and if it was to help the OWI sell the war to the people. For many years Americans had been attracted to popular song and dance – on stage, in movies, at ballrooms, and over the air waves. All these platforms of amusement continued unabated, ever growing to meet the public demand: almost half of Hollywood's more than 300 wartime films were musicals which combined escapism with patriotism. Walt Disney led the industry's animators to sell the war message via his cartoon characters, but also to produce a cartoon rendition of Alexander de Seversky's polemical book on strategic bombing, Victory Through Air Power.

The public needed a reaffirmation of the American dream – home, family, mother's apple pie, and all that victory promised. Hollywood provided that through a portrayal of sweet innocence and noble virtues on both the home and fighting fronts. To accomplish this, the message had to be repeated and exaggerated, leaving no doubts in the minds of Americans. So the entertainment industry omitted references to battles lost, racial discrimination, striking workers, blatant propaganda, or anything else which might bring wartime practices into question. Such inconsistencies in American society had to be glossed over in favor of projecting an unsullied, righteous, and unified America. Wartime was not the time for bold social experiments, nor for solving longer-term paradoxes. For America's cause was a just one, the Japs and Nazis were evil, and the republic had to be painted a lily white if the vast majority of people were going to defend it to the hilt.

Thus the movies and radio endlessly ground out the message "V for Victory," and people listened at home or went to the movie theater, which was now equipped with new-fangled air-conditioning and became a refuge of light in towns and cities otherwise darkened by civil defense blackouts. Before long, no fewer than 90 million people patronized movie

houses each week! The usual radio programs from peacetime continued with undiminished popularity, augmented by wartime specialties like the weekly Command Performance U.S.A., also transcribed and set overseas. The New York theater district lent its time and stars to the Stagedoor Canteen for servicemen on leave in the Big Apple, an example emulated by the Hollywood Canteen, founded by film stars Bette Davis and John Garfield. Servicemen mixed sex and sweetness in their choice of the top pinup, blond actress Betty Grable, whose fabulous gams (legs) were insured for $1 million. No matter that she was already married (to band leader-trumpet player Harry James); she was the flesh-and-blood realization of the fantasized Varga and Petty pinup drawings which adorned Esquire magazine. For sheer sex appeal, however, the troops preferred Rita Hayworth.

The movie industry needed no prodding from the government to promote democracy and condemn fascism as soon as Hitler had plunged Europe into war. In 1940 Frank Capra heralded the triumphant American individual with his *Meet John Doe* and *Mr. Smith Goes to Washington*, while Charlie Chaplin poked fun at the strutting *Great Dictator*, and Joel McCrea and Laraine Day only incidentally fell in love as German bombs rained down in *Foreign Correspondent*. The Jewish heritage of the movie moguls only added to a general pro-intervention stance by Hollywood, as depicted in Samuel Goldwyn's sobering anti-German film *Pastor Hall*. Movies reflecting the mobilization theme proliferated, but so did the unabashedly pro-Allied *A Yank in the R.A.F.* and especially *Sergeant York* in 1941. Isolationist Senators Burton K. Wheeler and Gerald P. Nye attacked Hollywood's bias in hearings but were thoroughly crushed by the defense counsel called in by the industry, none other than Wendell Willkie. The film that most awakened Americans to the menace of Hitlerism was *Confessions of a Nazi Spy* – followed closely by the real tragedy in the Pacific, the attack on Pearl Harbor.

Hollywood lost no time in reflecting the public's hysteria over the shock of the attack. It turned out *Little Toyko, U.S.A.*, depicting that section of Los Angeles as a den of Japanese agents. The movie was so blatantly racist against Japanese-Americans, even though they had been herded into the relocation camps, that Elmer Davis' OWI henceforth involved itself in monitoring all movie scripts. If America's war was a just one, a conflict of, by, and for the people, then films had to reflect fairness and proper balance. Nevertheless, the military reverses of 1942 caused filmmakers to stereotype the Japanese as tools of the devil himself – and often used actor Richard Loo to frighten audiences with his menacing demeanor, backed up by armies of Filipino extras in Jap garb. Serious movies turned a delicate balancing act between artistic realism, soft propaganda, and entertainment appeal as reflected in the sensitivities of the moguls, the critics, and the OWI. Spencer Tracy and Katherine Hepburn, the favorite romantic team of the era, came on as politically too strong in *Keeper of the Flame*, while the perfectly coiffed nurses of Guadalcanal looked just too artificial in *So Proudly We Hail*. The complex political intrigue of *Casablanca* worked with the careful juxtaposition between duty and love for Humphrey Bogart and Ingrid Bergman. Two best selling books which successfully painted good- vs evil themes worked less well as films – Ernest Hemingway's *For Whom the Bells Toll* on the Spanish Civil War of the late-1930s and John Hersey's *A Bell for Adano* about the Italian campaign. If these bells were not enough, Bing Crosby rang religious themes in *The Bells of St. Mary's* and *Going My Way*.

The plethora of combat flicks could not compete for sheer audience appeal with the musicals, comedies, and hometown themes. *Since You Went Away* touched the strains of an American family's travails most effectively, and Bud Abbott and Lou Costello typified the outright silliness attractive to civilians in need of laughs. The men and women in the field quickly outgrew such shenanigans but never failed to appreciate the personal appearances and good fun of Bob Hope and his overseas troupe, which always included one girl-next-door warbler, usually Frances Langford. The film title *Star Spangled Rhythm* reflected an entire genre of toe-tapping patriotic extravaganzas, the master maker of which was America's premier songwriter Irving Berlin. As if his one epic-melody

"God Bless America" was not enough, in early 1942 he cranked out the most enduring song-and-dance movie of the war – Bing Crosby and Fred Astaire in *Holiday Inn*, then used Army troops and Ronald Reagan in the dazzling 1943 epic *This Is the Army*. Unlike the smash Broadway musical *Oklahoma!*, *This is the Army* included a notable place for black performers, but strictly segregated, and all-Negro films like *Stormy Weather* – based on the life of dancer Bill "Bojangles" Robinson – and *Carmen Jones* were huge successes. *Stage Door Canteen* dramatized wartime separations, and linked music by big bands with cameo appearances by acting greats, and gave special attention to each U.S. ally, notably the Chinese. *The North Star* dramatized Russia's and *Mrs. Miniver* Britain's heroic stands against Hitler's legions, but Hollywood's attempt to promote the internationalism of the late (and taciturn) Woodrow Wilson missed the mark.

In many ways, Hollywood could be both mature and absurd in treating the war. From 1943 on, documentary films presented sobering realism that was great art as well as entertainment. Frank Capra produced the docu-series *Why We Fight*, focusing on the foot soldier, and an AAF bomber and a Navy aircraft carrier were portrayed vividly in *Memphis Belle* and *The Fighting Lady* respectively. Even certain dramatic offerings succeeded in approaching the real thing, like the plight of the PT boats struggling in the beleaguered Philippines in *They Were Expendable* and the Ernie Pyle-inspired *Story of G.I. Joe* in the European theater. In contrast, absurd were the specters of turn-of-the-century Sherlock Holmes à la Basil Rathbone projected into wartime America hunting Nazi spies, and Western singing cowboy stars like Roy Rogers figuratively lassoing the krauts on the range. The all-time low among much-touted films was Howard Hughes' *The Outlaw*, minus any war theme, much less competent acting, but high on Jane Russell's compelling full figure. And cynicism began to creep onto the silver screen as returning veterans and disoriented civilians became mired in the confusion of an uncertain future – the film noire of the postwar letdown.

Beyond the movies were the usual leisure attractions of books, art, music, and sports, and though gasoline rationing prevented vacation trips, people enjoyed circuses, war bond rallies, and parades which came to town. Best-selling novels, modern art, and symphonic music were not particularly reflective of the wartime environment and thus not intrinsically distinctive. The great war-bred literature would come after the return to peace: for example, Norman Mailer's *The Naked and the Dead*, Harry Brown's *A Walk in the Sun*, and William Wister Haines' *Command Decision*.

Athletics, however, suffered by the absence of the best professionals in the service, especially those of the national pastime, baseball, notably sluggers Hank Greenberg and Joe DiMaggio in the Army, pitcher Bob Feller in the Navy, and the last .400 hitter Ted Williams as a Marine Corps fighter pilot. Many old-timers kept the major leagues in business, however, like 35-year-old Spud Chandler, whose right arm brought him a 20-4 win-loss performance and the New York Yankees the 1943 pennant and World Series victory over the St. Louis Cardinals. In search of youth, the crosstown St. Louis Browns desperately employed one-arm outfielder Pete Gray in 1945 (he hit .218 in 77 games), while the Cincinnati Reds hired 16-year-old Joe Nuxhall to pitch in 1944 (he lasted less than one inning, walking five and giving up two hits). In college football, the military academies monopolized the best physical specimens, and of those West Point's Doc Blanchard and Glenn Davis dominated the sport. There was tragedy, too, for fun-seekers, as in July 1944 when a big-top circus tent at Hartford, Connecticut caught fire and collapsed, killing 167 children and adults.

"V for Victory" began as American's war slogan months before Pearl Harbor, a simple Churchillian motto to remind Americans of their duty and to sustain their morale. Glenn Miller's ace arranger Jerry Gray composed a hot instrumental number entitled "The Hop" during the autumn of 1941, quickly retitled "V for Victory Hop" to reflect the nation's preparedness. Such symbols lifted spirits otherwise dashed by Pearl Harbor and by repeated early defeats. In spite of full-employment defense spending, the New York Stock Exchange plummeted, with

AMERICA AT WAR

middle class confidence below the worst Depression lows; in March 1942 some 420,000 stocks changed hands daily. Then, with the first victories in the Pacific and the Allied landings in North Africa, confidence returned, and small investors began to pump up the market by the end of the year. Complaints from Marines over the inadequacy of their bayonets in the jungles of Guadalcanal even caused San Franciscans to mail them daggers more conducive to hand-to-hand combat. Global offensives during 1943 improved this optimism, no more dramatically illustrated than during an auction at Gimbel's New York department store when comedian Danny Kaye received a war bond pledge of $1 million for one of Jack Benny's beat-up violins. The donor was an unknown Julius Klorfein, the very quiet owner of a popular nickel-cigar company.

1944 dawned brightly, not only due to the belief that victory now seemed certain, but because The Leader, Franklin Roosevelt, called upon Congress to enact an "Economic Bill of Rights" to help all Americans fulfill their dreams of a good job, a comfortable standard of living, a decent home, fair trade practices, adequate medical care, an education, and general security in sickness and old age. These were high ideals, the epitome of the liberal American conscience, but too vague without a definite program to implement them. Indeed, such a blueprint did exist – the New Deal. Placed on the back burner by "Dr. Win-the-War," FDR's social programs seemed to him applicable to the new world adawning. He would need the support of Congress, but that support had been slipping ever since the Congressional election of 1942 had brought to Capitol Hill a phalanx of Republicans determined to dismantle the old extravagant Depression era agencies. The specter of cradle-to-grave social security smacked of socialism, hardly attractive in the midst of the economic boom being directed by the captains of industry. One by one, the old New Deal agencies died for lack of Congressional funding, while wartime bodies or their heads got the ax on the often questionable charge of obnoxious mismanagement, notably Leon Henderson of the OPA, Donald Nelson of the WPB, and the entire domestic arm of the OWI.

Roosevelt's vision of guaranteed economic rights therefore gained adherents in only one respect – social security for the returning veterans. Congress in 1943 initiated the idea of rewarding the men then waging and winning the greatest war in history, an opportunity which FDR seized late that year by calling for a "G.I. Bill of Rights" – subsidized postwar education and unemployment benefits. With 1944 an election year, and under pressure from veterans groups, Congress accepted the challenge and hammered out the Servicemen's Readjustment Act, enacted into law in June 1944. This so-called G.I. Bill guaranteed college or trade-school tuition, books, and subsistence funds, as well as business and home loans and the underwriting of medical expenses in veterans hospitals. It was a triumph for the country, even if the overall "economic bill of rights" never reached fruition, for 8 million veterans would receive direct aid in the immediate postwar period – a healthy shot in the arm for the national economy and for colleges decimated by the war.

Overall, the political mood of America was swinging to the right. People always tire of crusades and self-sacrifice – witness the Roaring Twenties backlash to Woodrow Wilson's Great War crusade for democracy. Victory became assured when the dramatic news of D-Day was trumpeted throughout the land on June 6, 1944 – the Allied landings at Normandy to begin the liberation not only of occupied France but of Hitler's entire "Fortress Europe." The desire for liberal change and social experimentation melted before a public craving for stability, conservatism, and a continued economic boom. FDR, ever conscious of public opinion, had organized labor on his side as well as solid political support in the South and most of the rest of the country. He had to handle alike the Congressional Republicans and his own Democrats, who were less interested in social change because he was the only viable candidate able to run on the Democratic ticket in November 1944.

A fourth term. Like the third, unprecedented, but this campaign solicited support from the majority of Americans, who had no stomach for changing heroes in the midst of the war. FDR cagily avoided active campaigning. He was too busy running the war in any case, and his

health was obviously not in top form; just how tired he was only his personal physician really knew. The Republican opposition differed little from the Democrats in its platform – win the war, continue the prosperity, and enact modest social reforms. The Wisconsin primary decided the G.O.P. candidate. Wendell Willkie had become too liberal for the old-liners and was soundly eliminated (then, sadly, he suffered a fatal heart attack). War hero Douglas MacArthur had a sort of passive political charisma but never played a part in the campaign and had his name withdrawn after a poor showing. Governor Thomas Dewey of New York garnered most of the votes in Wisconsin and soon became the Republican nominee. Then, in a subtle but decisive political move, Roosevelt allowed the Democratic convention to dump the candidacy of the arch liberal Henry Wallace for renomination as Vice President. Instead, the safer Senator Harry Truman got the nod; his investigations of wartime agencies had made him an honest, attractive, if somewhat lackluster, figure. In a word, Dewey never had a chance – unless the war ended before November. It did not, and FDR won again handily.

The plain fact was that, by November 1944, Roosevelt had become nothing more than the trusted war leader in a conflict that was nearly finished – at least in the minds and attitudes of the American people. After four years of restricted travel and rationed consumer goods, people were flocking back to race tracks and bowling alleys, breaking out their tuxedos and evening gowns to attend concerts, using their bloated savings to buy jewelry and black-market nylons, and frolicking at late-night bistros and bars as cities began to relight their streets for lack of offshore U-boats or visions of transoceanic enemy bombers. Advertisers promised automobiles, refrigerators, and even television in the near future, and industrialists pressed the WPB to allow them to begin large-scale reconversion. People were so tired of tending Victory gardens that they responded to a government call to increase the number above the current 18 million by allowing many to fall into disuse.

December 1944 changed all that. Hitler's legions launched a massive counterattack at the Allied armies on the Western front, halting them for over a month in the bloody Battle of the Bulge. American leaders and citizens were stunned. Already suborbital V-2 rockets had begun plunging into London and liberated cities on the continent, creating visions of longer-range missiles crossing the Atlantic to hit New York (which in fact the Germans were developing). At the same time, the Japanese initiated a furious attack of kamikaze suicide planes against Allied naval forces in the Pacific – an ominous stratagem which the U.S. government kept from the public for several months. Nor did it comment on the appearance of Japanese high-altitude, bomb-laden "Fugo" balloons which had just begun to descend over the American West; one killed a half-dozen persons on a Sunday-school outing in Oregon the following May. Not only was the war not over, but the military estimated that Japan would not be beaten at least until the invasion occurred in 1946.

As long as such doubts over achieving an expeditious victory existed, the government could use national defense as the pretext for new directives. When 1945 began, therefore, FDR ordered a nationwide cutback in reconversion plans, a midnight curfew at all public places, and the closing of racetracks. The people did not accept this new call for sacrifices. It simply did not ring true, for it wasn't. The Army and Navy understandably feared a weakening in war production and resolve, and FDR had had to acquiesce as their commander in chief. Within three months, however, the European and Pacific offensives had resumed their inexorable march, and the government lifted the curfew. The interruption had done little more than anger the people sufficiently to flaunt the rules and keep the party going – they had merely wolfed down the booze faster to hang one on before midnight.

Public disquiet lay deeper than this brief interlude. Servicemen were already returning in large numbers to be discharged under an elaborate point system based on length of time in combat and family responsibilities. To be sure, they were given well-deserved heroes' welcomes, and most returned to normal lives as typical citizens. But some turned bitter toward civilian brethren who appeared insensitive to their sacrifices. Worse, the presence of permanently maimed and mentally wounded

veterans in the midst of material-minded civilians who had been physically unscathed by the war increased public guilt. The teenagers who had left teenage-level jobs came back as men disinterested in such former hum-drum positions. Many could not adjust and turned to crime or to a lifetime of frequenting Veterans Administration hospitals. Others never did completely reconcile themselves to the workaday world; their experiences of intense camaraderie and give-and-take under fire had obviously given them, as the postwar movie said it, *The Best Years of Our Lives*.

More difficult for the people to accept was the revelation of the Holocaust – Hitler's wanton massacre of the Jews, as many as 6 million by the time all the figures were compiled. A prewar isolation-minded public had refused to open the doors of immigration to the 1938-39 refugees of Hitler's persecutions, most tragically the merchant ship *St. Louis*, whose 907 German Jews were turned away to return to Europe (most, however, being admitted by friendly nations). Though the government began to learn of the atrocities in 1942, the information was withheld from the general public, prompting Jewish organizations to hold a mass rally at New York's Madison Square Garden in mid-1943 to urge the government to address the problem of rescuing Jewish refugees. The State Department official responsible for immigration, Breckinridge Long, resisted, largely because he was an avowed anti-Semite, like many Americans suspicious of successful Jews in American society. Secretary of the Treasury Morgenthau, the only Jew in the cabinet, and Eleanor Roosevelt, that great and good friend of the oppressed, took up the cause and won the support of the new Under Secretary of State Edward Stettinius, Jr. In January 1944, therefore, FDR created the War Refugee Board to help European Jews, but when the first of them arrived from liberated areas at centers like Oswego, New York, they were merely disparaged as "Eleanor's Folly." Then, in the spring of 1945, newsreels began to show the emaciated victims at the concentration camps freed by the Allied armies. A stunned public would take years to fully grasp and comprehend the incredible horror of the Holocaust.

On a broader scale – the restoration of a war-ravaged Europe – the United States was more active, initiating a study committee late in 1942 and then the United Nations Relief and Rehabilitation Administration (UNRRA) in agreement with 43 other nations the following May. It came into being that November, with former New York Governor Herbert Lehman as director general. Such international cooperation extended to Congress, which passed resolutions during 1943 to create and join an official permanent United Nations for the postwar world – a goal strongly advocated by FDR and Secretary of State Cordell Hull. Few Americans objected, for future world wars had to be prevented at all costs, but they wanted American interests protected. The first step was a meeting with British delegates at Bretton Woods, New Hampshire, during July 1944. There, the Americans, led by Henry Morgenthau, established an international monetary fund and bank to reconstruct postwar Europe with American funds. Great Britain, already weakened by its heavy war expenditures and heavily dependent on Lend-Lease, could only yield to U.S. leadership. Secretary Hull and the American business community wanted a free trade policy to assure postwar economic supremacy at the expense of a shattered British Empire. American postwar pre-eminence could not be doubted, but few realized that Britain would then collapse as a great power, leaving America to restore Europe virtually alone.

The political aspects of the proposed United Nations were the subject of a meeting of the four major Allied powers at the Dumbarton Oaks estate in a suburb of Washington between August and October 1944. There, Under Secretary Stettinius – about to replace an ailing Cordell Hull – met with representatives of Britain, Russia, and China to hammer out the working draft of the United Nations charter. In general, their blueprint laid the basic foundation, but a great many specifics were left unresolved. FDR went to the Yalta conference early in 1945 where the Allied heads of state agreed to convene the first meeting of the United Nations on April 25. One of the conditions for membership was a state of war between each U. N. nation and Nazi Germany, whereupon the United States convinced still-neutral Latin American countries like Argentina to declare war. Optimism soared in an America on the verge of victory and ready to establish a new and safer postwar world. FDR's fourth inaugural address in January set the tone: "We have learned that we cannot live alone at peace, that our own well-being is dependent on the well-being of other nations far away. We have learned that we must live as men, not as ostriches...."

Hitler's armies were in full retreat, the Atlantic Allies under Eisenhower pressing into Germany from the West, the huge Red Army from the East. Big B-29 bombers were raining incendiary bombs onto Japan's cities, while the Pacific Fleet landed an army on Okinawa. All seemed well enough to assure confidence in the future, when, on April 12, like a personal stab in the heart of every American, Franklin Roosevelt suddenly died at his summer home in Warm Springs, Georgia. The universal disbelief could only be compared with the shock over the Pearl Harbor attack. The nation staggered under the weight of genuine grief. The Leader was gone, an era disappearing with him.

But the pause to honor him proved short, for events proceeded at a dizzying pace. The new President, Harry Truman, seemed ill-suited for the task of filling such immense shoes, but he plunged headlong into finishing FDR's job by ordering that the San Francisco U.N. conference proceed. On April 25 the talks began, although they soon ran into difficulties as the Soviet Union balked over questions of membership for pro-communist states. Then, the first week in May, Hitler committed suicide, and on the 8th Germany surrendered. V-E Day: Victory in Europe. Americans went wild, but Truman kept pushing the crucial U.N. issue by dispatching Harry Hopkins to Moscow to work out the problems with the Russians. They had promised to declare war on Japan, and their manpower would probably be needed for the final invasion. Hopkins convinced Joseph Stalin to compromise on several issues, paving the way for the final signing of the U.N. charter on June 26. The President sent it to the Senate for ratification, which was easily obtained.

The summer of 1945 became a strange period between war and peace. While troops began to be redeployed from Europe to the Pacific, many generals came home for parades watched by tumultuous crowds. So this five-year-old future historian sat on a wall one block from his home in San Gabriel, a suburb of Los Angeles, to see the hometown hero pass down the street – General George S. Patton. He even addressed the Sunday school class of his old church, and mine – the Church of Our Savior. But, of course, I had no idea of what it all meant. President Truman journeyed to war-torn Berlin in mid-July to hammer out the final ultimatum to Japan and discuss the postwar world with the British and Russians. On the way back, he issued the order to use the atomic bomb on Japan. The news of its dropping on Hiroshima and Nagasaki in early August electrified the nation and the world. No less important was the simultaneous Russian declaration of war against Japan and its stunning attack on the Japanese armies in Manchuria.

One week later, August 15, I was going about the business of any fun-loving American kid – splashing about in a neighbor's small canvas wading pool – when the sound of sirens began to fill the air. Mothers came running out of their homes with the news – "The war is over! The war is over!" I will never forget it. Japan had surrendered, and my father could end his long, hard, and often sleepless days and nights of toil as a shipyard electrician for the Bethlehem Steel Corporation on the Los Angeles waterfront. Instead of going back to his prewar job as a butcher, he would join the ranks of war-weary Americans to seek the fulfillment of his lifelong dream, which he did – as a successful golf professional and businessman. And my mother would stop kneading food coloring into oleo cakes and saving the fat drippings from her meat dishes for the war effort.

The official V-J Day – Victory over Japan – occurred on September 2, 1945 when the Japanese signed the surrender documents on board an American battleship in Tokyo Bay. The celebrations continued unabated as the boys – and girls – came home. One of my uncles returned from carrier duty on an admiral's staff, another from service as a Navy dentist, another from playing drums in an Army band. And we all got on with living our lives – my own just beginning and with my very first memories being of America at war.

AMERICA AT WAR

The emotional response of the American people upon entering World War II had not been unlike that of a long-unemployed man who has suddenly found a good job: he gratefully turns to the work at hand with alacrity, determined not only to perform well in order to stay on the payroll but to do so well that he will be promoted. Such a simile is not far-fetched, considering the impoverished state of Depression America's economy on the eve of the war, a national psyche bruised and relatively aimless. The war changed all that, renewing Uncle Sam's confidence in himself as he rolled up his sleeves and found renewed vigor with a fresh and noble purpose – to eradicate fascism, the greatest scourge the modern world has known. The tireless democrat not only outperformed all the other workers around the globe to achieve final victory but ended up as the boss, a result he had never seriously entertained at the start but which he was forced to accept as the war progressed.

Before the fall of France in 1940, the United States had failed to realize its national potential. The American dream had been torn asunder by the Depression, casting serious doubts over the very viability of free institutions (democracy) and free enterprise (capitalism) in a world of dictatorships. From the earliest colonists three centuries before, Americans had nurtured an almost religious belief that we were the Chosen People, the beacon on the hill of hope for the world's oppressed. Our great Civil War had bound up the nation's political divisions, but the social and legal contradictions had not been resolved in the seven decades thereafter. The nation had been decisive in saving Europe in 1917-18 but also unwilling to face up to its peacetime responsibilities as a permanent and leading member of the family of nations. It had looked the other way while fascism spread and only began to accept reality after France gave up and Britain stood alone.

Pearl Harbor in one fell swoop changed America forever. With sudden finality, the Japanese woke up Americans with a painful, crippling right to the jaw. The shock of such recognition of a new reality comes only once to a great people, and a syndrome of fear over another sneak attack became the cornerstone of all subsequent U.S. policy toward the outside world. With sharp clarity, the people and their government united as never before or since to teach Germany and Japan, as Winston Churchill remarked at the time, "a lesson the world will never forget." Whereupon the United States made itself into the arsenal of the democratic spirit everywhere and armed to the teeth to crush evil with just and righteous cause. For a nation of pragmatists, it became only common sense to pull out all the stops – even to the point of unleashing the cosmic powers of the atom against the foe.

To Americans' self-image of vastness of land and spirit, the war added the ultimate bigness of all aspects of American life, not just for the duration but forever – big government, big business, big science and technology, big agriculture, big labor, big education, big armed forces, big fun, and big problems – which required big answers. New Deal or no, Franklin Roosevelt enlarged the power of the federal government so greatly that it would never be able to contract again, no matter which political party predominated, or whoever happened to occupy the White House.

Such a mammoth four-year transformation of American society was so swift, massive, and unanticipated that mistakes, waste, and pettiness infected most political agencies – not least Congress. The urgency to win prevented fine tuning or sober long-term planning. Mistakes could best be nullified by sheer productive output. It led to a relentless overkill, but it worked. If federal agencies did not police themselves sufficiently – and most didn't – then at least the specter of the vicious enemy foe made everything all right. "Don't you know there's a war on?" America's long-awaited destiny was being fulfilled in this singular crusade; let history be the final judge.

If the return of prosperity during the wartime economic boom seemed incongruous, or even a bit self-righteous, the vivid memories of deprivation and social injustice in the Depression era kept the crusade in its proper perspective. That, and the tens of thousands of Americans who died on foreign soil, in foreign skies, across endless seas, and at hazardous industrial plants right at home – and widows, gold star mothers, fatherless children, and interrupted or terminated dreams. At bottom, the war was serious business, and everyone pulled together in common effort. They were proud of their achievement, and the rest of the world never underestimated it or them.

In victory, however, came the illusion of omnipotence, that the United States by its sheer willpower and superior arms had guaranteed the success of the postwar peace. Yet, within months of V-J Day, the Soviet Union had clamped an Iron Curtain across central Europe, Chinese Communists began the drive which would overthrow our allied Nationalists, and the British, French, and Dutch empires quickly evaporated to nationalistic native movements. Over the course of the first decade of "peace," the two superpowers squared off in the thermonuclear Cold War, America rearmed to rescue western Europe for the third time, and a tenuous *Pax Americana* settled over the globe as the United States dictated and enforced international law. The real illusion was our belief that we could rest on our laurels after the Victory. The bittersweet truth soon taught us that our great crusade had unleashed to the masses of the world the same force that had won the war – democracy. Having fathered it during the war, we were in no position to abandon it, however unruly the process of democratization became.

World War II in fact taught the harsh lesson that peace and war could not be treated as separate historical phenomena. The dollar-a-year industrial managers and the uniformed strategic planners had to be perpetuated in formal governmental agencies – the National Security Council and Department of Defense forged during 1946-49. No more could amateurs be appointed to high strategic office; the business of maintaining the peace and engaging in wars became continuous under professional leaders. The wartime arrangement became the model for the military-industrial complex of the future. America's long adolescence was over. We had no choice but to mature as a superpower.

So too did the not-so-young republic have to answer its internal contradictions forced into the open by the war: racial and ethnic inequities, the refusal to accept Rosie the Riveter into the permanent work force with equal pay and opportunity; inadequate social security for all economic classes; and – above all – the need to respect and genuinely understand all peoples of the world for what they are and not what we would like them to be. None of these pressing matters could have been resolved during the heat of wartime, but when that ended they could no longer be ignored. To be genuine, the American dream had to embrace all the people. Decades of turmoil since then have yet to find complete or satisfactory answers – but the war started the ball rolling.

Finally, wartime America shaped an entire generation to surge confidently into the future, to meet challenges frontally as it had between 1941 and 1945. The memory of that supreme collective achievement was fixed in the hearts and minds of the veterans of the fighting fronts and the home front to the end of their days. The postwar era has long since ended, the old animosities are spent, the fears over an inevitable – or even possible – World War III dissipating. Democracy is breaking out virtually everywhere, a revolution set in motion largely because of the American victory in World War II – and the legacy it left of the United States overseeing the peace ever since.

Without that Victory, forged by the American people, the new era beckoning on the horizon of the 21st century would not be possible.

Behold the American coed of 1940! Long, flowing hair was only starting to inch up to the shorter convenience style of the war years. Blue jeans were becoming the rage for their sheer comfort, although the Marlene Dietrich influence kept slacks in vogue.

1939-40

New York City's Board of Education initiated its own preparedness measures as part of the National Defense Emergency Training Program in September 1940. These youths, in casual dress as well as suits and ties, registered for one or more of 26 special courses offered to help prepare them for possible military duty.

1939-40

PRELUDE TO WAR

After ten years of the harshest depression in its history, America celebrated a fresh hope for the new decade with the New York World's Fair. Such optimism quickly proved premature, however, when in September 1939 Adolf Hitler's *Wehrmacht* blitzed into Poland to begin World War II. At first, the conflict appeared to be a "phony" one, as Allied Britain and France made no major moves against the Germans. Most Americans consequently affirmed their supposed isolation from Europe's squabbles and looked forward to new model cars and other material possessions denied them since the 1920s. Then, in the spring and summer of 1940, Hitler suddenly conquered Norway, the Low Countries, and France.

The danger could no longer be ignored, so while the people and their representatives in Congress debated whether to become involved in the war, the government took steps to aid the British – now under aerial siege by the *Luftwaffe* – even as the nation rearmed for its own defense. Congress authorized a two-ocean navy, not only to protect the Eastern seaboard but to deter the increasingly aggressive empire of Japan in the Pacific. President Franklin D. Roosevelt was re-elected on the promise to keep us out of the war, but just one month later – December 1940 – he pledged to turn America into the "arsenal of democracy."

The music which Americans enjoyed in movies, on records, and over the radio reflected both the confidence of an invigorated nation and a romanticism due partly to doubts about the future. The swing era peaked with Artie Shaw's challenge to Benny Goodman as clarinet-playing King of Swing, while the new orchestra with the widest appeal, Glenn Miller's, enabled jitterbuggers to jump while "In the Mood" and dreamy lovers to embrace to his theme song "Moonlight Serenade." Boogie woogie jazz piano became all the fad – "Beat Me Daddy, Eight to the Bar" – and frenetic Harlem drummer Chick Webb suddenly died but bequeathed to the world his band's marvelous vocalist, Ella Fitzgerald. "God Bless America," sang Kate Smith, and young Judy Garland looked "Over the Rainbow." Cowboy singer Gene Autry was glad we were "Back in the Saddle Again," and Walt Disney's cartoon movie *Pinocchio* made the future look bright "When You Wish Upon a Star."

But the 1940 tune "This Changing World" said it all by asking where the world was taking us, and what it meant. One conclusion appeared unavoidable – we were going somewhere different and not just in the movies with Betty Grable *Down Argentine Way* or with Bob Hope, Bing Crosby, and Dorothy Lamour on *The Road to Singapore*.

PRELUDE TO WAR 1939-40

That many Americans could foresee the approaching calamity was amply demonstrated on the night of September 23, 1938 when collegians of the American Student Union paraded through New York City's Times Square to protest Nazi Germany's bloodless absorption of Czechoslovakia's Sudetenland during the Munich crisis. To appease Hitler's threats of war in Europe, the British and French governments allowed *der Fuehrer* to take possession of the German-speaking Sudetenland on the promise to leave the rest of Czechoslovakia alone. Theater-goers stopped to watch and even cheer the marchers, who obviously had the "Great War" of 1914-18 in mind by donning gas masks in fear of what another world war would bring. (Thankfully, poison gas never appeared in World War II.) Six months later, Hitler effortlessly marched into Czechoslovakia proper, and on September 1, 1939 – less than a year after the student march – he invaded Poland. Americans would ignore the Nazi threat only at their peril.

When the New York World's Fair opened on April 29, 1939, the uncompleted Czechoslovakian pavilion was a solemn reminder to Americans that the Czech nation – a hyphenated republic in existence only since World War I – had been absorbed into Hitler's empire. The Czech flag is seen flying at half-mast on the right, the American flag above and behind it as a tour bus rolls by. New York Mayor Fiorello La Guardia immediately defied an order from Prague barring the exhibit by forming a committee to complete it. The pavilion opened on May 31, Dr. Eduard Benes, former Czech president, declared at the Fair's Court of Peace that his nation would never give up the struggle to regain its lost liberty. But "the tempest of wrath" recalled from the 17th century Czech educational and religious reformer John A. Comenius would not pass even with the eventual defeat of Germany; Soviet troops remained on Czech soil until 1990.

"The World of Tomorrow," conceived by planner Robert Moses, attempted to make the New York World's Fair a popular vehicle for imagining a future America. The Electric Utilities Pavilion let visitors walk through the cascading waters that generated the hydroelectric power already transforming rural America through the New Deal's Tennessee Valley Authority (TVA). But the giant gears in the background were mechanically only a cut above the imaginary space ships of Buster Crabbe's movie serials as Flash Gordon and Buck Rogers. Indeed, General Motor's *Futurama* portrayed a super city whose centerpiece was nothing less than a dirigible base – this only two years after the fiery crash of the *Hindenburg* at Lakehurst, New Jersey had sealed the fate of passenger airships. The outbreak of war in Europe in September 1939 caused the Fair's operators the next year to soft-pedal a technological tomorrow in favor of patriotic hoopla and a small-town aura more in keeping with Norman Rockwell's folksy *Saturday Evening Post* magazine art. Hitler's blitz that spring caused the Fair and the future to be set aside indefinitely.

The Fair's giant money changer of the National Cash Register company affirmed the late President Calvin Coolidge's telling remark back in the 1920s that "the business of America is chiefly business." Although the Franklin Roosevelt administration was less pro-business in 1939 than it had been during the early New Deal five years before, the economy had since recovered sufficiently to inspire a new confidence and the Fair itself. No matter that the two-year extravaganza proved to be a financial bust. This immense cash register bears an architectural resemblance to an escapist Busby Berkeley movie set – the sleek art deco vogue of the Depression Thirties. In late 1940 design genius Frank Lloyd Wright, after a long absence, returned to the forefront of American architecture. Decrying such starkness in favor of warmth and integration with natural landscapes, he ushered in a new look for the America of the Forties and after.

PRELUDE TO WAR 1939-40

William O. Douglas poses in his robes on April 17, 1939, the day he took the oath as an associate justice of the U.S. Supreme Court. A feisty liberal, Douglas had helped shape FDR's New Deal by checking the power of Wall Street financiers through the Securities and Exchange Commission (SEC). In the mold of the judge he succeeded, the eminent Louis D. Brandeis, Douglas stood firm and loudly for individual rights against the corporations. Although a champion of the Bill of Rights, he shared the reluctance of the entire Court in wartime to protect civil liberties of persons arrested for dissenting against the war effort. All were still chastised by the memory of FDR's recent attempt to "pack" the Court with his own men to support New Deal laws. Douglas' and the Court's liberalism would not soar until after the war. A rags-to-riches figure, he had been raised by his mother, a widow, worked his way through high school and college in the state of Washington, and, hobo-style, rode the rails in a box car to reach Columbia Law School in the early 1920s – the same time that Lou Gehrig was there as an undergraduate.

Nobel laureate physicist Albert Einstein had fled Nazi Germany in 1933 to become a professor at the Institute for Advanced Study in Princeton, New Jersey, where he labored to develop a unified field theory explaining the nature of the universe. His ingenious mathematics were so complicated that he often stumped fellow scientists, as here during a lecture in Pasadena, California during which he turned to find his listeners utterly baffled at his equation on the blackboard. The originator of the theory of relativity, he had brought luster to the American scientific community and a powerful voice for peace and international cooperation. While he and his colleagues began to unlock the secrets of the stars, they realized that this very force could be duplicated in the laboratory for the creation of a bomb of incredible power. Fearing the Nazis might mobilize German scientists to create such a weapon, Einstein wrote a letter to President Roosevelt in 1939 warning of the possibility. This action set in motion the sequence of events that led to the Allied construction of the atomic bomb during the war, during which Einstein acted as a consultant to the Navy. His unified field theory never achieved success, but Einstein remained the symbol of American science the rest of his life.

PRELUDE TO WAR 1939-40

"The Iron Horse" of baseball, the national pastime, Lou Gehrig took himself out of the New York Yankees lineup on May 2, 1939 after having played a record (which still stands) of 2,130 consecutive games since 1925. Typical of America's self-image of power, virility, and selflessness, "Larruping Lou" had played first base for the Yankees in the shadow of his colorful teammate Babe Ruth while quietly clobbering the opposition with a lifetime .340 batting average, 493 home runs (including four in one game), and 1,991 runs batted in, along with .361, ten homers, and 35 RBIs in seven World Series. Faltering at the end of the 1938 season, the 35-year-old Gehrig managed to scratch out only four hits in eight games before benching himself at the start of the 1939 season. Tragically, this gentle hero had been stricken with a rare fatal paralyzing disease that now bears his name and was hurriedly inducted into the Baseball Hall of Fame. America wept when he said farewell at Yankee Stadium on July 4, on which occasion he reflected that his happy life and dazzling career had made him "the luckiest man on the face of the earth." The nation mourned his death in June 1941, the year in which Gary Cooper faithfully portrayed him in the film biography *Pride of the Yankees*.

The craggy face of radio comedian Fred Allen matched the voice that millions of Americans encountered on "Allen's Alley." Seen here trying out a few gag lines on youngsters at the National Broadcasting Company's talent school in 1939, Allen and his writers tickled the funny bones of their listeners with caricatures of the ethnic and regional types that inhabited the land. There was his own wife, Portland Hoffa, the inevitable Jewish mother Mrs. Nussbaum, and the cracker-barrel hayseed Titus Moody, but especially the quintessential Southern politician, Senator Claghorn, who boomed out the puns — "I was glad to see Senator Aiken back! (laughter) Achin' back! That's a joke, son! (More laughter)" — the target being Yankee George Aiken of Vermont.

PRELUDE TO WAR 1939-40

If pimply teenaged boys grew muscles on the Charles Atlas plan, it was because they fantasized over attracting ideal femmes like movie sex goddesses Marlene Dietrich. Though she was famous for her legs, the very idea of those curvy limbs could be evoked even behind the women's slacks she had already made famous off camera by the time she first appeared in them on camera in this scene from the 1940 film *Seven Sinners*. Her alluring gaze tore into the soul of many a man-boy, accentuated by a sultry song in her customary low tones as in this scene. A hat rakishly tilted over one eye never failed to add to her mystique, even when it was a U.S. Navy lieutenant's cap – a hint of the growing military imagery as war neared. Marlene's manner evoked the high class of a Hollywood which continued to "put on the Ritz" just as Fred Astaire and Ginger Rogers had done bedecked in tux and gown for endless dazzling film dance sequences. Dietrich may have been the daughter of a German cavalryman, but she hated Nazis and scored her biggest wartime triumph with a grueling, whirlwind tour of American military bases and forces in the Mediterranean during 1944-45.

The very best of them all, and backed always by the cream of jazz musicians on the New York scene, Billie Holiday sang jazz and the blues. She was a Negro, which mattered not at all to the Caucasians who heralded her musical genius in an age when racial segregation reigned in all walks of American life – except among jazz musicians. Black and white jazz players shared musical ideas at informal jam sessions and on phonographs backing her unique, warm, and full-toned voice as she sang the lyrics by slightly but perfectly staying just behind the beat. Dubbed "Lady Day" by tenor saxophone giant Lester Young (whom she named "Prez" for "the president" in reciprocation), Billie usually appeared in public wearing a big flower in her hair as in this 1940 New York "gig" performance. Hard years of racial abuse and frustrated loves led her into drugs and alcohol – and repeated bouts with the law – but she never wavered in her music, which included several songs that she composed herself. "Strange Fruit" and "Fine and Mellow" were her hit tunes of 1939 and "Lover Man" in 1944, when she won an *Esquire* magazine jazz award. Billie Holiday epitomized jazz singing – then and ever since.

Father Divine (George Baker) had emerged during the Depression as a black messiah and "Dean of the Universe," so flamboyantly preaching and practicing peace that he crossed racial lines by also attracting white followers to his crusade. Women disciples were his "angels," seen here parading through Harlem at the end of the 1930s to celebrate the purchase of 500 acres on the Hudson River north of New York City as their new "heaven." Harlem was the major center or "Peace Mission" of his movement until he returned to Philadelphia, that city of brotherly love, in 1942. Although he was regarded as a buffoon or con man by detractors, Father Divine's appeal for nonviolent change blended democratic and pacifistic ideals that spoke to the needs of many aimless Americans. He commanded headlines in 1939 and thus surprised many blacks by condemning the totalitarian societies of Nazi Germany and the Soviet Union after they carved up Poland that year. And in a January 1940 sermon he lauded the American political system as the best in the world; racial prejudice could only be overcome by individuals. Father Divine's hatred for the Nazis deepened in 1941 when Hitler cited his crusade as an example of American racial integration. He viewed the Allied cause as a crusade for freedom and equality and claimed America's moral strength to be more important than its military power.

The passage of the Selective Service Act on September 16, 1940 meant that a draftee would have to go into the Army, usually considered less glamorous than the Navy, Marines, or Army Air Corps. This restriction did not seem to bother these young men who, one week later, stood in line three ranks deep outside New York's Whitehall Street recruiting building to volunteer for the Army. Held in check by one of "New York's finest," these youngsters – including a few blacks – endured construction work to smile and mug for the camera as they rallied to the call. Note the brick pavement, which still typified some of the city's older streets.

Republican Presidential candidate Wendell L. Willkie delivers a whistle-stop speech from the rear of his twelve-car campaign train at Modesto, in California's central valley, September 22, 1940. An opponent of the New Deal but a confirmed liberal, the dynamic Hoosier corporate lawyer obtained the G.O.P. nomination against a dozen opponents in June partly through efforts of nationally-organized "Willkie Clubs." By the time he reached Modesto, he was near exhaustion. At the start of the swing through the Midwest two weeks before, he had rejected the use of a loudspeaker and with his typical flamboyance tried to project his voice over the first throngs he addressed. His voice quickly gave out, and a throat specialist was able to restore it only partially. Accepting the microphone, Willkie still had a gravel-like delivery as he gestured with powerful sweeps of his arms and a tossed lock of hair over his forehead.

Endorsing America's entry into the war, the stocky, five-foot-two Father Divine spoke often and fervently at meetings like this one and at war bond drives, defending both conscientious objectors and persons who elected to fight for their country. Indeed, he predicted that one day the United States would lead humanity away from enemy "isms" in the cause of liberty, equality, and justice. This patriotic stance clashed with that of many other black leaders who saw little difference between Nazi and American racism.

Black veils of mourning adorn nine mothers of sons of military age who opposed the mobilization. The moms sit in the reception room of the U.S. Senate as a "death watch," opposing the conscription bill in August 1940; they even burned pro-draft Senator Claude Pepper in effigy. Organized into the Mothers of the United States of America, these ladies, mostly from the Cleveland area, were the vanguard of many women en route to the nation's capital to sit in silent protest while Congress debated instituting the draft. "They feel," said vice president Rosa M. Ferber of Detroit, "that it is their duty to protect their sons from the horrors of war."

1941

Crowds in Times Square watch the moving lighted bulletin board on the New York Times building flash the news from the Pacific the night of December 7, 1941. A soldier anxiously holds an evening tabloid announcing the outbreak of war, for all military leaves are now cancelled, the futures of the GIs uncertain. The civilians seem more interested in smiling for the camera, unfazed by the light rain, but also perhaps already fatigued by the steady stream of shocking news ever since early afternoon.

1941

AMERICA AT WAR

The debate over isolation versus intervention in the European war intensified as military and industrial preparedness created a national prosperity on an unprecedented scale. Jobs for skilled and unskilled workers, women and teenagers, urban and rural whites and blacks brought steady paychecks to more Americans than even the pre-Depression era had known. But the boom also upset the even tenor of American life, as job seekers migrated to cities with defense plants, and the military swelled with patriotic enlistees and the first peacetime draftees in the nation's history. Fat war contracts revitalized business with such immense earnings that the labor unions struck for higher wages and safer working conditions. The government encouraged John Q. Public to invest in America's security by buying defense bonds, while civil defense measures inspired community groups to stand ready should the war spread to America.

The fighting did spread to America's waters, gradually in the Atlantic but very suddenly in the Pacific. As Hitler's U-boats attempted to clamp a submarine blockade around the British Isles, FDR strengthened America's ties with the former mother country and instituted transatlantic convoys escorted by U.S. Navy warships. The Anglo-American military connection became so strong that in May the President declared an "unlimited national emergency" and thereafter waged a quasi-war against German subs. Then in June the Germans invaded Soviet Russia, even as Benito Mussolini's fascist Italians attempted to gain control of the Mediterranean Sea and North Africa. Japan made World War II truly global when its sneak attack on Pearl Harbor, Hawaii, sank the American battle fleet on December 7. A stunned America ended the year faced with the Herculean task of having to fight and eventually defeat the Axis powers.

"I Got It Bad (and That Ain't Good)" was Duke Ellington's 1941 tune that could have been applied to America's post-Pearl Harbor shock. By then, the people were already mourning the fate of Europe with "The Last Time I Saw Paris," but had also begun to sing about their own preparedness in tunes such as Irving Berlin's "Any Bonds Today?" Comics Abbott and Costello frolicked their way through movies about all the burgeoning armed services – *Buck Privates*, *In the Navy*, and *Keep 'Em Flying* – and were accompanied by the Andrews Sisters warbling over the "Boogie Woogie Bugle Boy" of Company B. Cole Porter wrote the music to which a uniformed Fred Astaire and Rita Hayworth danced in *You'll Never Get Rich*. Not the G.I. (Government Issue) troops perhaps, but the expanding middle class did well enough to buy that "String of Pearls" celebrated by Glenn Miller. The road back from Pearl Harbor would be a long one, although Hope, Crosby, and Lamour had already taken another cinematic road trip of their own – to Zanzibar in East Africa, of all places.

AMERICA AT WAR 1941

Franklin Delano Roosevelt moved from peerless domestic leader to dynamic wartime commander in chief during the turbulent year of 1941. At his right hand, politically and literally in this scene, was Harry Hopkins, veteran social reformer and shrewd New Deal manager who terminated his secretaryship of commerce in 1940 to move into the White House as FDR's closest confidant. Physically frail from cancer and stomach ulcers, Hopkins nevertheless accepted the position of Lend-Lease coordinator for war materials to Great Britain in 1941 and remained near the center of wartime diplomacy. The President, seen disembarking from his yacht *Potomac* at Rockland, Maine for a rest at his Campobello hideaway in August, was rarely photographed with his leg braces in view. His bout with polio in mid-life had left him a paraplegic, whereupon news photographers had extended him this courtesy. Rarely also was he ever pictured propped up with cane and a supporting arm, in this case provided by his straw-hatted naval aide, Captain John R. Beardall (who spent the war as Superintendent of the U. S. Naval Academy).

The bulging power of America's most powerful magnates was captured in the Academy Award-winning best film of 1941 — *Citizen Kane*. A production of the brilliant Orson Welles, seen also in the starring role, this epic movie set the hollow materialism of great wealth in stark contrast to the high spiritual idealism of an America preparing for war. Charles Foster Kane, though fictional, seemed so closely modeled after newspaper tycoon William Randolph Hearst that Hearst's influential movie gossip columnist Louella Parsons urged RKO studios not to release the film after she had seen the preview. RKO hesitated, then let it out to an admiring public. In many ways, this specter of crass, corrupt, and power-hungry business leaders devoid of love and feeling served as a sober reminder that truer and higher virtues guided the American dream and the mobilization of industry for a noble crusade. As motion picture art, however, *Citizen Kane* employed cinematic techniques that were innovative and prophetic, making it one of the greatest films of all time.

King of Swing Benny Goodman was still "riding high" (the title of one of his instrumental numbers) in 1941 at dance halls, hotel ballrooms, over the radio, and at theater concerts like this one. Once the band started to "jump," jitterbug dancers would clog the aisles to release their energies. Although challenged by rival clarinetist Artie Shaw, Benny rebounded from having lost "name" sidemen like trumpeter Harry James and drummer Gene Krupa, who formed their own orchestras, by forging what many critics still regard as his best band—that of 1941-42. It featured new, innovative arrangements by Eddie Sauter as well as upgraded chestnuts from Fletcher Henderson, and soloists included Mel Powell on piano, Vido Musso on tenor sax, trombonist Lou McGarity, and trumpet player Cootie Williams, as well as girl singer Peggy Lee.

No motion picture moved America more to the Allied side during 1941 than *Sergeant York*, a true-to-life biography of Tennessee farm boy Alvin C. York who overcame a deep religious pacifism to fight for his country in World War I. The real-life York insisted only that the actor who portrayed him be Gary Cooper, an admired, shy person himself who played similar roles in *Meet John Doe* and as Lou Gehrig in *Pride of the Yankees*. That Cooper succeeded in the difficult role of portraying a person still living was recognized by his Oscar for best actor of the year. York/Cooper was entirely believable wrestling with his conscience to accept the Augustinian dictum that a man must fight for home and hearth whenever there is "a clear and present danger." He was equally admired for using his backwoods marksmanship in one action to pick off 20 Germans with his rifle and lead the capture of 132 others and their 25 machine guns – the very image of the frontier minuteman conquering the professional armies of Europe and for which York received the Medal of Honor. A gala opening at the Astor Theater in New York on July 1 was accompanied by a parade down Broadway by York and a meeting with the President.

AMERICA AT WAR 1941

"This in London calling," Edward R. Murrow intoned over the transatlantic underwater radio cable to the firesides of the average American home. With air raid sirens moaning in the background, punctured by the dull thud of antiaircraft bursts and crashing bombs, Murrow bravely and quietly conveyed the full meaning of the Nazi scourge from the first day of the war to V-E Day. In so doing, he elevated the science of radio broadcasting to a high literary art with his minor creations of colorful, incisive and yet spontaneous accounts of the drama which unfolded about him. He conveyed what he regarded as the Britishers' "degree of casual confidence, courage and courtesy which is remarkable" to the American people. Murrow's personal delivery of the news from Europe became a major tool in welding the wartime Anglo-American peoples in common cause.

Boogie woogie music had been all rage in the two years preceding this March 1941 jam session of the University of Minnesota Boogie Woogie Club. The creation of Kansas City-based black piano players – notably, by 1941, Meade Lux Lewis, Albert Ammons, and Pete Johnson – this offshoot of hot jazz and traveling (railroad) music rollicked with eight beats to the bar instead of the standard four, the steady rhythm laid down by the pianist's strong left hand. The white orchestra led by Will Bradley built on the boogie piano of Freddie Slack to produce many hits, especially "Beat Me, Daddy, Eight to the Bar." This collegiate trio wrote and here performs "Beat Me Dimitri" for its specially invited guest, Dimitri Mitropoulos, conductor of the Minneapolis Symphony Orchestra. After hearing it, he protested boogie to be monotonous and superficial. So it was, the fad already starting to die out, although these students seem to be listening intently enough.

Luxury ocean liners like France's huge 83,423-ton *Normandie* criss-crossed the Atlantic until the coming of the war ended the age of the great passenger liners forever. After the fall of France in the summer of 1940, the *Normandie* was interned with these three French freighters in New York harbor. This picture was taken on March 31, 1941, the day that the Roosevelt administration seized all German, Italian, and Danish vessels in American ports because the government expected the "emergency" – American entry into the war – momentarily. The U.S., however, did not finally claim the *Normandie* until December 12, following Germany's declaration of war. Two weeks later the Navy renamed her *Lafayette* and began her conversion into a troop transport.

On February 9, 1942, the *Normandie/Lafayette* caught fire from a welder's torch and quickly turned into a blazing inferno. Firefighting boats can be seen trying in vain to play sufficient water on her stern during that wintry day. Three hours past midnight, she capsized, settling on her side into the harbor mud. The Navy did not give up and in a massive salvage operation managed to right her again on August 7, 1943. Hoping to convert her into a combination transport-aircraft ferry, the Navy placed her in a dry dock two months later, only to discover her damage too extensive and shipbuilding manpower too critically strained to proceed.

On May 1, 1942 President Roosevelt purchases the first defense saving bond from Secretary of the Treasury Henry Morgenthau to kick off the huge campaign to stimulate revenues for wartime production.

AMERICA AT WAR 1941

The "midget Army reconnaissance truck" or "blitz buggy" were names given in this March 1, 1941 photograph to what soon became famous as the "jeep." The very first one of the initial 1,500 to come off the Ford assembly lines at Dearborn, Michigan is demonstrated digging through wood chips, aided by snow chains around the tires. Passengers Edsel Ford and Brigadier General Charles H. Bonesteel seem to be enjoying the ride The four-wheel drive, with six forward speeds and two in reverse, gave the four-cylinder motor great adaptability and maneuverability in rugged terrain. The ubiquitous jeep became one of America's most useful pieces of military hardware for this war and others yet to come.

Patriotic automotive magnate Henry Ford (facing page, third from right), donated a five-acre tract and buildings for a naval training school in Detroit. He and son Edsel Ford (right) welcome a Navy delegation for the formal opening of the facility on January 17, 1941. Standing next to the senior Ford is the Chief of the Bureau of Navigation, responsible for naval training, Rear Admiral Chester W. Nimitz, who eleven months later would resume command of the Pacific Fleet.

The great Ford automotive complex around Detroit joined the other auto makers in taking over much of the country's production of airplane engines. Here (left), in August 1941, Major General H.H. "Hap" Arnold, Chief of the U.S. Army Air Corps (left), and Henry Ford (arms folded) inspect the model of a new supercharged in-line V-type 12-cylinder liquid-cooled aircraft engine.

The sharing of aircraft contracts with auto makers was no more dramatic than when San Diego's Consolidated company – merged with Vultee to become Convair early in 1942 – turned to Henry Ford to join in the production of its four-engine B-24 Liberator bombers. Ford employees are seen (below) in September 1941 at their old plant learning to make B-24s.

AMERICA AT WAR 1941

America's unofficial entry into World War II may be said to have occurred the last week of May 1941 when President Roosevelt declared an "unlimited national emergency" upon the breakout of the German battleship *Bismarck* to attack North Atlantic shipping. He feared that American vessels might be sunk and thereby force the United States to retaliate. The fate of the *Bismarck*, however, is displayed on a bulletin board in New York's Times Square on May 27; her consort, *Prinz Eugen*, escaped to Brest, in occupied France. New York businessmen could refer to the bulletin board (right) to learn of the events of the European war, including British losses in the Mediterranean. From this day on, U.S. ships and planes cooperated with British forces in tracking German submarines in the "Battle of the Atlantic."

As the U.S. Army gradually built up a strength of 1,400,000 men between the passage of the Selective Service Act in September 1940 and the summer of 1941, it made certain that all its inductees were physically qualified – with an A-1 designation – and not bad physical risks to send into combat. Thus these early draftees are given pre-induction physical examinations at New York's 71st Regiment National Guard Armory to ascertain whether they can pass the actual induction physicals. If so, they can plan to separate themselves from civilian life for one year. If not, as 4-F rejects they need not interrupt their jobs. By September 1941 the deepening of the war in Europe and the deterioration of Japanese-American relations in the Pacific led the Army to extend the term of service for its draftees.

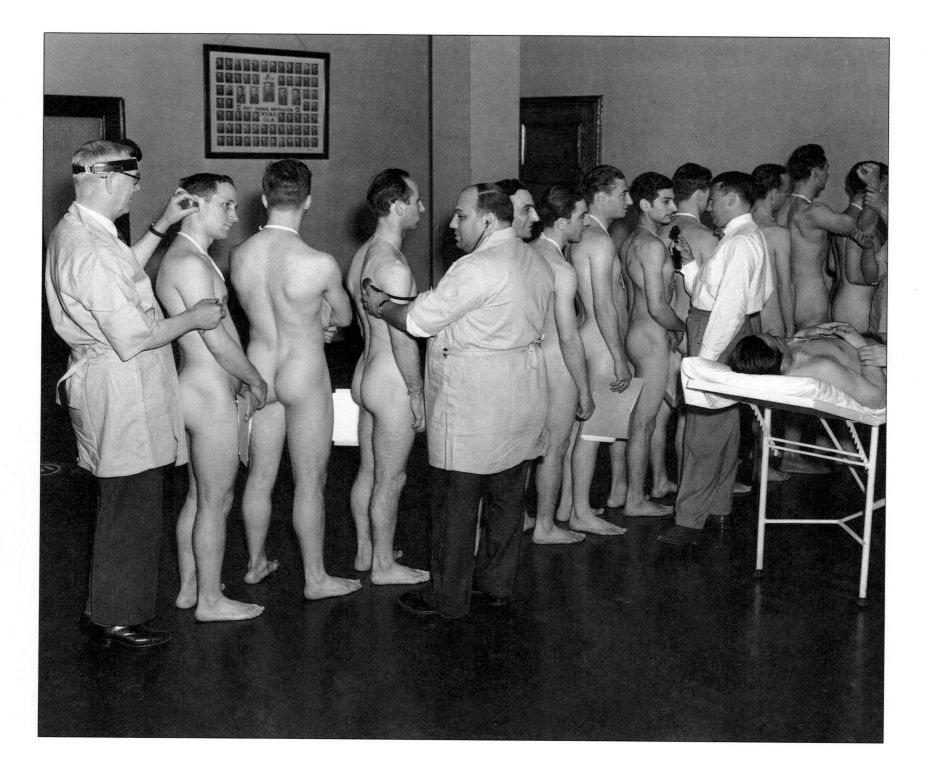

AMERICA AT WAR 1941

Being kissed goodbye was one of the pleasures of an advertised departure to the wars—but especially by a movie starlet. Here, in March 1941, an Army first sergeant gets a taste of Martha O'Driscoll, who is held up by a private, while a corporal anxiously waits his turn and a rather older looking "buck" sergeant stands behind the Army truck. These infantrymen are moving with full field gear — backpacks, sheathed bayonets, canteens, ammunition belts, holstered pistols, leggings, and Springfield bolt-action rifles. Such statewide units (like this Company "E" as the guidon standard shows) trained in the World War I-vintage rifles until the new Garand M-1 could be issued to them.

Dancing cheek-to-cheek in front of the jukebox is this new soldier's way of spending his first Army paycheck on February 2, 1941. He was one of 16,000 men training at Camp Bowie, one of dozens of hastily-constructed army camps throughout the country, this one located near Brownwood in central Texas, southwest of Ft. Worth. The total payroll at the camp on this date was $1,250,000. Why he is dancing with his cap on – and with a rain cover on it to boot – is a mystery.

Small-town America, especially in the warmer South and West, was transformed whenever a military installation popped up nearby. Modern-day camp followers descended on such towns, and the morals of soldiers and local girls were easily loosened in the emotion-packed freedom of wartime. The United Service Organizations provided wholesome recreation to counter such temptations, as in tiny Winnfield, Louisiana, where, in September 1941, the U.S.O. sponsored a block dance on the main street. Although the local base was Pollock Field, central Louisiana was home for several Air Corps bases and Army camps and the scene of much-publicized peacetime maneuvers that year. The music here is provided by 108th Infantry's band of the 27th Division. Private Neil Simon later captured life in such Southern camps in his play and film *Biloxi Blues*.

Anxiety over a possible German air attack on the East coast led some institutions to begin preparing air raid shelters as early as March 1941 – like the Allerton House hotel in New York City. In the "sub-basement" 45 feet underground, four women guests sample the makeshift shelter with hot plate, kerosene lantern, Spartan furnishings, the latest *Time* magazine, and a patriotic reminder of the probable necessity for such sacrifices. The portable lantern reveals doubts about the boast in the original caption: "An auxiliary lighting system has been installed in case the hotel's own light plant goes out of order."

Civilian employees of the Navy Department in New York's airports, storehouses, and shipyards try out the latest type of gas mask at the Naval Clothing Depot early in 1941. None of the men see any humor at all in the dreaded prospect of ever having to endure a poison gas attack from the sky. The only real scare over that possibility – a clear violation of an international law to which all the warring powers had agreed – occurred during the summer of 1942 when the U.S. and Japan made counter claims that the other might employ gas. Residents of West coast cities remained alert to the danger for almost a year thereafter, but it never materialized.

AMERICA AT WAR 1941

"Blackout" drills were organized in American cities throughout 1941 on the model of London, which had to remain completely darkened at night lest enemy bombers pick out a point of aim. Boy Scouts in New York practice first aid on a make-believe victim, using their neckerchiefs as blindfolds to simulate conditions during a blackout. "Be Prepared" was their motto, and they practiced it in this Maytime exercise.

Not to be outdone, Girl Scouts show themselves equally adept the same day, perhaps to specialize treating the wounded in daytime bombings – for their neckerchiefs remain in place. The city-wide event of several Scout troops drew an interested crowd of onlookers.

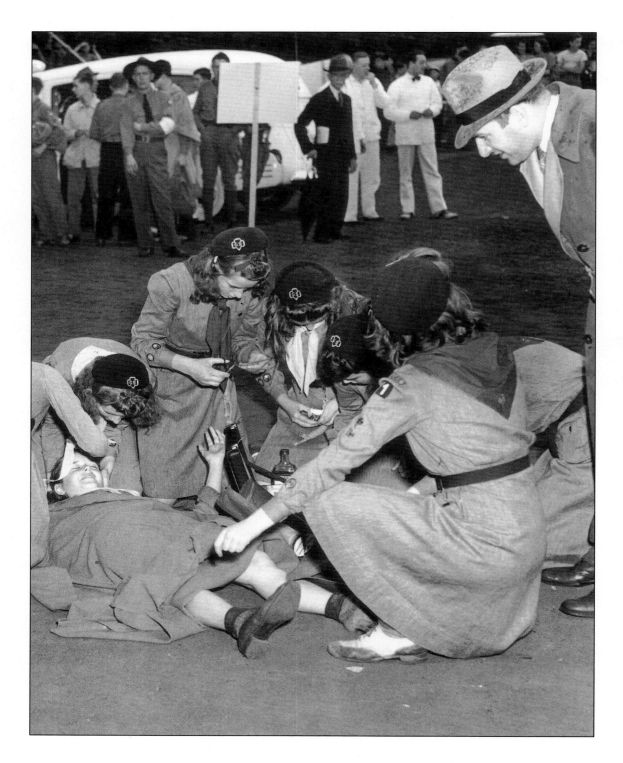

AMERICA AT WAR 1941

Aircraft plant security intensified along the West coast during the year to guard against the possible dual threats of sabotage by Japanese agents and air attack by Japanese planes. Inasmuch as Japan had launched a sneak attack on the Russian fleet without a declaration of war at the beginning of the century, the War Department was taking no chances. These two Army gunners man a .50 caliber water-cooled antiaircraft machine gun atop the Consolidated Aircraft Company factory in San Diego in June 1941. In the event of a surprise raid, they would have plenty of help from the Navy guns and planes located in the San Diego-Los Angeles area.

Ground Observer Corps units mobilized in several states during 1941 under War Department control and as part of the Air Corps' Aircraft Warning Service, assisted by the American Legion. The one atop the new Nassau County Courthouse in Mineola, on New York's Long Island, is manned by four Sea Scouts and two Legion members on December 8, 1941, the day after the Pearl Harbor attack. These warmly-clothed spotters – like most, manning unsheltered observatory platforms – augmented the Office of Civilian Defense (OCD), created under the leadership of Mayor Fiorello LaGuardia of New York but too loosely organized to be taken seriously until the shooting actually started. In December the Civil Air Patrol (CAP) of privately licensed pilots turned up to augment Army and Navy reconnaissance planes along the coasts – eventually reaching 80,000 men and women members, some of whom actually bombed and sank German U-boats, a few at the cost of their own lives. Another 20,000 teenagers took CAP pre-flight training. Also, the OCD improved markedly after war began, its wardens and countless numbers of Americans quickly learning to identify aircraft.

Fiorello LaGuardia, the "Little Flower" of New York, boasted of the OCD's readiness for war but devoted most of his efforts toward public relations in reassuring Americans of their security. This inspection of newly-designed utility aprons for potential women civil defense workers in June 1941 is one example. The First Lady of the land, Mrs. Eleanor Roosevelt (right), assists him here and on similar occasions, although they don't seem too pleased with one another. Six months later, on December 7, both of them were inspecting West coast OCD preparations, and when La Guardia learned of near panic in his own city over unidentified planes (U.S. Navy, as it happened), he announced, "This is the time to speak frankly. So frankly, nowhere in this country is civilian defense operating to my satisfaction." He then moved with alacrity to make up for lost time.

AMERICA AT WAR 1941

Patriotism notwithstanding, organized labor had no patience with corporation executives who gleaned ever-greater profits from war contracts without passing commensurate increases to workers' wages as the costs of living rose. Following steel, auto, and shipyard strikes, the C.I.O. called a walkout of 9,000 aircraft workers at North American Aviation in Inglewood, southern California on June 5, 1941. The government reluctantly gave in to the workers' demands, but profits continued to mount throughout the war and with them the strikes. These North American strikers wanted, and got, a ten cent per hour pay hike.

The United Auto Workers of the C.I.O. struck the Ford company's River Rouge plant near Dearborn, Michigan, in April 1941, thus stopping production on all of the many defense contracts at the Ford plants. Four years before, the U.A.W. had struck at the same place and been bloodied by Ford's security guards. As this well-dressed young man (left) walked through the main gate, he answered the boos of the pickets by offering to "fight anyone of you." They close in on him at once, pummeling and pushing him up against a car fender. But the rough-and-tumble days of physical employer-employee battles were numbered. Just as Henry Ford had been a pacifist in World War I and had now decided to help arm his country for war, he also shelved his rule never to bargain with unions and agreed to negotiate. The victory enabled the U.A.W. to organize every auto maker.

Miners' boss John L. Lewis (below at right) personified organized labor in 1941, although his trademark billowing silver-flecked hair and bushy black eyebrows are masked behind his hat as he crosses a C.I.O. picket line in 1942. Repeated United Mine Workers strikes in 1941 angered the rest of the nation, but his supreme self-confidence remained so unshaken that the next year he defied C.I.O. president Philip Murray over the latter's preference to cooperate with the administration in the war effort. But Lewis hated FDR, and Murray was also a vice president of the U.M.W. Underestimating Murray's solid support within the rest of the C.I.O. – as evidenced by this poster – Lewis sacked Murray from the U.M.W. and then took the union out of the C.I.O. altogether. The flamboyant, colorful leader remained a thorn in the side of the President, but his influence over organized labor declined after this dramatic move.

Thousands of auto workers at Ford's River Rouge plant return to work on April 14, 1941 after successfully renegotiating their contracts. Although most Americans resented the unions' refusal to work in spite of national defense needs, the general complaint of organized labor was legitimate: war profiteering was bloating the pockets of their bosses. After a hard decade of Depression, managers and workers alike had no intention of suffering again. Notable among the throng here are a great many blacks, many of whom had migrated from the rural South and who were gradually accepted into the unions.

AMERICA AT WAR 1941

Aviation hero Charles A. Lindbergh – the first pilot to fly solo across the Atlantic, in 1927 – speaks before an America First rally at Philadelphia in 1941. This Committee, organized in September 1940, dominated the field of several isolationist groups campaigning to keep the United States out of the European war and even rejecting aid to the British. Centered mainly in the Midwest, at that around Chicago, the A.F.C. lobbied long and hard and exploited Lindbergh's considerable image to pave the way. But as the mood of the country swung toward intervention, the America Firsters lost prestige, especially as the Lindbergh inarticulately fumbled and distorted his own position. When the President impugned his loyalty, a stung Lindbergh resigned his Air Corps Reserve colonelcy. And in a September 1941 speech at Des Moines, Iowa he intertwined his sympathy for the oppressed Jews of Germany with their being a key force behind America's pro-Allied stance, making him appear anti-Semitic. In fact, as an airman, he had been so impressed by Hitler's air power that he did not believe any nation could stop it in Europe – though he seemed to ignore the strategic implications of his own transatlantic flight. His wife Anne Morrow Lindbergh had written *The Wave of the Future* in 1940, that "wave" being fascism. Discredited after the Des Moines speech, Lindbergh withdrew from the debate, but just as quietly became a civilian consultant for the wartime Army Air Forces and on an "inspection" tour in the Pacific shot down at least one Japanese plane in combat.

Anti-German feeling intensified in June 1941 when the F.B.I. smashed a Nazi espionage ring in the United States. For more than a year, naturalized American citizen William Sebold, recruited as a German spy, allowed the F.B.I. to bug and film (through a one-way mirror) his New York office as his fellow agents revealed their activities. J. Edgar Hoover's agents rounded up 33 suspects, the last one, Gustav Wilhelm Kaerchner (facing page at left), having been leader of the pro-Nazi German-American Bund unit in Staten Island until 1938. Sporting a Hitler-style mustache, Kaerchner pleads not guilty to chief assistant U.S. attorney T. Vincent Quinn (right) in Brooklyn's Federal Building, the very same place where he had been naturalized as an American citizen ten years before.

Unlike Kaerchner, most of the other spies, including one woman, when arraigned here in Brooklyn before U.S. commissioner Martin G. Epstein on June 30 pleaded guilty. Each was jailed on $25,000 bail bond on charges of espionage and failing to register a foreign agent, a major blow to Hitler's prestige in America. Their arraignment before a Jewish magistrate was an added if fortuitous insult to these agents of the so-called "master race," whose glum demeanor is broken only by the smiling lawyer in the foreground. Exposed by the surreptitious film footage during the dramatic trial which ran from early September till mid-December, all were found guilty and given sentences of up to 18 years. William Sebold's reward for acting as a double agent was anonymous protection by the F.B.I. in an undisclosed part of the country.

Speaker of the House of Representatives Sam Rayburn signs a bill repealing the last vestiges of American neutrality on the Atlantic sea lanes, November 13, 1941. Throughout the year, U.S. naval vessels had convoyed unarmed American merchant ships to a point at mid-ocean where British warships took over for the final run-in to English ports. Under earlier neutrality acts, no U.S. merchantmen were allowed to carry deck guns, but recent U-boat attacks on American cargo ships required some protection. So the House agreed after a bitter battle on the floor led by two Democratic Congressmen who revolted against Sam Rayburn's majority, Howard W. Smith of Virginia and Lansdale G. Sasscer of Maryland (right). But the bill passed, 212 to 194, under the direction of Democratic Whip Patrick J. Boland of Pennsylvania (far left) and Majority Leader John W. McCormack of Massachusetts (second from left). By the time the bill became law, America was in the war.

In October 1941 the U.S. government established an alien internment stockade (below) at Camp Upton on Long Island for spies like those captured in New York and for enemy nationals after the official declarations of war. This stockade was simply another subtle example that American entry into the war was only a matter of time.

Facing page: American soldiers and sailors give the gals of the U.S.O. stage show *Razzle Dazzle* a sendoff at New York's Penn Station, December 1, 1941. Unknown to the happy G.I.s and chorines, the last days of official peacetime were slipping away.

To buy time for arming in the Pacific, the Roosevelt administration gladly agreed to discuss Japanese intentions with two emissaries. FDR specifically wanted a clarification of reported Japanese troop movements in French Indochina, the Vichy French colony already occupied by Hitler's Asian ally. Japan sent special envoy Saburo Kurusu (facing page at right) to join the Japanese ambassador, Admiral Kichisaburo Nomura (left), in explaining this and Japan's general conduct in Asia. The two men are seen talking with reporters as they arrive at the State Department for one of several meetings with Secretary Cordell Hull over several days, this one on December 5, 1941. They had already presented what amounted to an ultimatum to the United States to unfreeze Japan's assets in America and to allow Japan to continue its war in China. In fact, the two diplomats were also buying time – to smokescreen the approach of the Pearl Harbor striking force. Two days after this picture was taken, the truth came out.

Broadway at 42nd becomes more than the heart of the "Great White Way" as the eyes of the world reciprocate the gazes at the bulletin board of these Americans suddenly plunged into the global maelstrom. The average American knew more of Manila than Pearl Harbor before this momentous day, thereby giving the Japanese air attack on the American Philippines equal weight with the Hawaiian disaster.

AMERICA AT WAR 1941

A grim-faced crowd in New York's City Hall Park listens to a loudspeaker broadcasting the President's message to Congress asking for a declaration of war on Japan. When he finished, they solemnly nodded in agreement.

Even the New York Stock Exchange halted business to hear the President's address at half past the noon hour as the clock shows. Among the attentive Wall Street brokers are those of the Bethlehem Steel Corporation at center.

Resolved by the Senate and House of Representatives of the United States of America in Congress assembled, That the state of war between the United States and the Imperial Government of Japan which has thus been thrust upon the United States is hereby formally declared; and the President is hereby authorized and directed to employ the entire naval and military forces of the United States and the resources of the Government to carry on war against the Imperial Government of Japan; and, to bring the conflict to a successful termination, all of the resources of the country are hereby pledged by the Congress of the United States.

Speaker of the House of Representatives.

H A Wallace
Vice President of the United States and President of the Senate.

Approved
Dec. 8 — 1941   4.10 p. m. E.S.T.
Franklin D Roosevelt

President Franklin D. Roosevelt, wearing a black armband in mourning for the nation's first war dead, signs the declaration of war at 4:10 p.m., Eastern Standard Time. The key Congressional leaders present seem pleased at America's defiant reply to Japan's aggression. Shown looking on are House Speaker Sam Rayburn, Vice President Henry Wallace, and Republican House Minority Leader Joe Martin of Massachusetts.

For a nation long accustomed to Roosevelt's fairly intimate "fireside chats" over the National, Columbia, and Mutual radio networks, the President returns to the microphones on the evening of December 9, 1941 to tell the people, "We are going to win the war and the peace that follows." The weight of his new responsibilities seems already to have taken its toll on the President.

Fearful of receiving a similar visit from the Japanese carrier armada, San Francisco was thrown into a state of extreme anxiety by the Japanese attack on Pearl Harbor. To disseminate air raid warnings, the music studios which operated phonographs by private telephone wires to some 500 jukeboxes at cafes, bars, and recreation centers granted use of their equipment to civil defense authorities. Four people at one such bar listen intently on December 12, 1941 to an announcement over one of the wired juke boxes which carried air raid warnings, "all clear" signals, and general civil defense information. Happily, no attack ever came, for the Japanese carriers were already heading west to support the invasions of Wake Island and the Dutch East Indies.

Southern California shared its northern neighbor's nervousness, especially the many oil wells located near the Los Angeles and Long Beach coastline. On December 14, 1941 an Army sentry polices one of the smaller derricks, ready to find cover behind a pile of sandbags. The wells dot the dry countryside, shared with, in this scene, a railroad crossing, meat market, filling station, cafe, liquor store, and billboard advertising California wine. Otherwise, life goes on in L.A.

AMERICA AT WAR 1941

Racial prejudice against Japanese-Americans mounted following the Pearl Harbor attack, as seen on this rural California store's swinging door.

To a packed House filled with Senators, Representatives, and gallery observers, Britain's Prime Minister Winston Churchill spoke the day after Christmas 1941. In spite of serious British and American losses in the Far East, this consummate master of the common English language started with an understatement that brought chuckles: "I cannot help reflecting that, if my father had been American, and my mother British, instead of the other way around, I might have gotten here on my own." The emotion building, he expressed astonishment that the Japanese, "in a single day, have plunged into war against the United States and the British Empire; they certainly have embarked upon a very considerable undertaking." And how! Then, he pronounced in restrained fury, "What kind of a people do they think we are? Is it possible they do not realize that we shall never cease to persevere against them until they have been taught a lesson which they and the world will never forget!!" Whereupon, to tumultuous applause, he held up his two fingers in the already-famous V-for-Victory sign. America had a second heroic leader.

1942

A volunteer sells war savings stamps to passersby from a sidewalk booth in front of a Whelan's drug store in New York. The portable phonograph apparently played music between the live music indicated by the drummer's cymbal in the lower right corner. It is early 1942, when "defense stamps" became "war stamps," as the updated poster on the bottom of the booth shows.

1942

AMERICA AT WAR

In the air age, which had already awakened Americans to the vulnerability of London to Hitler's bombers and of the U.S. Navy to Japanese carrier planes, the prospect of an attack from the skies frightened most of the people during the early months of their war. Blackouts of all lights darkened American cities as the people girded for the air raids which in fact never came. The immediate danger, more subtle since it could not normally be seen, lay in the U-boats which ravaged U.S. and Allied merchant shipping along the Eastern seaboard and within the Caribbean Sea. The loss of the goods these vessels carried added to the shortage of raw materials theretofore obtained by America and Allies from Southeast Asia—notably rubber and oil. Rationing, therefore, gradually impinged on the lives of all Americans as voluntary scrap drives failed to provide the quantities of these strategic raw materials necessary for the war effort.

The war raged throughout Europe even as Japan overran the Philippines, Malaya, Burma, the Dutch East Indies, and the Pacific islands. The feeble American and Allied forces were virtually annihilated trying to defend these places and to shore up an embattled China, already at war with Japan since 1937. Although the Soviet Union remained neutral in the Pacific, convoyed American goods were rushed to Russia and to Britain to bolster these nations' resources against Germany and Italy. Successive American defeats in the Pacific were dramatically halted by the battles of the Coral Sea, Midway, and Guadalcanal, though the cost was so great that only increased industrial output could guarantee the American stand at the latter island. Finally, in November 1942, American forces landed in Axis-held Morocco, North Africa, and American submarines began to penetrate Japanese waters to sink that nation's merchant shipping.

Here We Go Again was the name of the film in which comedians Fibber McGee and Molly stated the obvious, but Hollywood proved equal to the new challenge with *Star Spangled Rhythm* and especially Crosby and Astaire in Irving Berlin's memorable *Holiday Inn*. Song and dance buoyed American spirits, with such big bands as those of brothers Jimmy and Tommy Dorsey laying down the beat. Even folks with two left feet could learn how, said the novelty tune "Arthur Murray Taught Me Dancing in a Hurry." But movies like *Song of the Islands* and the Hope-Crosby *Road to Morocco* belied the harsh wartime conditions in those now-unromantic places. "Don't Sit Under the Apple Tree (with Anyone Else But Me)" pleaded the departing loved ones, for someday "We'll Meet Again." And the people sang for strength: "Praise the Lord and Pass the Ammunition" and "Remember Pearl Harbor." Or they laughed, along with Spike Jones' City Slickers, right in "Der Fuehrer's Face." But as Duke Ellington's fine jazz tune put it, "Things Ain't What They Used to Be." Of course, they never are.

Surrounded by sandbags for protection against bomb fragments and aerial strafing, two gunners man an antiaircraft gun within sight of the Lincoln Memorial and Washington Monument – one of many scattered AA guns placed in entrenchments and atop buildings throughout the nation's capital immediately after the declarations of war against Japan, Germany, and Italy. Although no Axis bomber then in existence could have flown the Atlantic and returned, and neither Germany nor Italy had aircraft carriers, Pearl Harbor had shaken American self-confidence. Rear Admiral John H. Towers, Chief of the Navy's Bureau of Aeronautics, tried to assure Congress that any air attack would be a mere "stunt," but his words fell on deaf ears for the first few weeks of war.

English musical comedy star Gertrude Lawrence donned armband and flashlight to serve as one of over 60,000 New York City air raid wardens. Married in 1940 to an American producer, she elected to adopt the U.S. as her new home and in 1941 achieved her greatest success in the Broadway play *Lady in the Dark*. And that she was – here telling the neighbors in Sector A, Zone 1, 18th Precinct to douse their lights. "CD" stands for Civil Defense.

AMERICA AT WAR 1942

As Mayor LaGuardia set to work streamlining the nation's civil defenses, he took no greater pains than with his own city. This New York volunteer answers one of several telephones in a large communications center as her supervisor looks on. At first, false alarms abounded, and confusion reigned. All of Manhattan went dark with its first blackout in April 1942, and auto accidents increased – a trend throughout the country. When lights were found inadvertently aglow, mobs would forcibly douse them before an air raid warden even arrived. By summer, however, calm returned due to the lack of any attacks, and civilian defensive measures became more systematic.

In a residential neighborhood of southern California's city of Long Beach, one block's Civil Defense team stands ready with its own emergency wagon, equipped with everything necessary to respond to an air attack: stretchers, fire extinguisher with long nozzle, large shovel, and garden hoses. Each warden has a special skill, though only the nurse seems to be properly attired. Despite the club-like spirit of the wardens, the date was June 8, 1942, only days after Japanese forces had landed in the Aleutians and attacked Midway in the Hawaiian group – potential threats to the West coast. This neighborhood is almost identical to the one in another Los Angeles suburb, San Gabriel, in which the author spent the war years (the first six of his life). Well remembered by him were the man next door as block warden, blackouts, and covered streetlight fixtures.

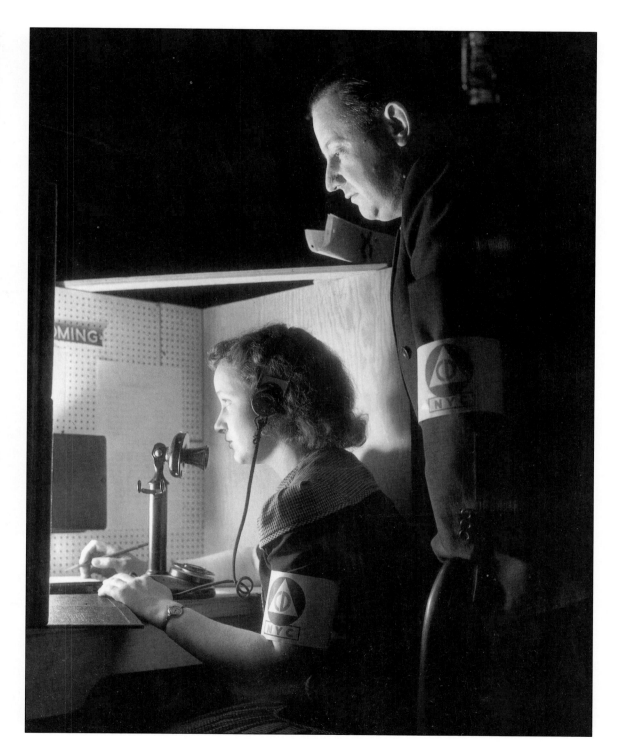

AMERICA AT WAR 1942

95

The 11,000 Local Defense Councils organized civil defense work at community level, including specialists like these New York City anti-gas wardens seen drilling in the cleanup of toxic debris. As recently as 1935, the film adaptation of H.G. Wells' fictional *Things to Come* had shown entire populations of cities being gassed during aerial bombings – fear of which persisted throughout World War II.

AMERICA AT WAR 1942

Defense plants constructed shelters for their workers, like this five-feet-wide tubular affair built of three-inch-thick concrete culvert pipe for Red Cross-trained women of the Vought-Sikorsky division of United Aircraft Corporation in Stratford, Connecticut. The entire structure was also cushioned by sandbags, and two ambulances with full-time medical workers stood on constant alert. The date of this picture is February 4, 1942.

Although LaGuardia was unable to build many air raid shelters even in his own city due to the need for vital building materials by defense industries, some were constructed. This shelter on New York's Lower East Side opened on July 13, 1942. Designed by students of the Pratt Institute's architecture department, it was a half-block-long space formerly used for recreation by a model tenement development. No less than 4,000 sandbags cushioned the foundation walls. At school, children held air raid drills during which they crawled under their desks.

A profit could be had in wartime emergencies, even from one of these New York City air raid shelter contraptions which retailed early in 1942 for $100. The 30-inch-high posts at each corner were purported to be capable of supporting a 35-ton load, presumably of bricks falling onto the steel top, while the wire mesh could stop all but the smallest pieces of flying plaster and splinters. But what to do in case of fires caused by enemy bombs?! These four "chicks" get their laughs modeling the expensive coop, but as vital a strategic building material as steel could not be spared for such contrivances, even if they had worked. By early 1944 everyone realized the enemy would never come to America, and civil defense measures fell into general disuse.

The U.S. Territory of Hawaii was home for 90,000 Japanese and 160,000 Nisei, or American-born descendants of Japanese – like sister and brother Miki and Kiuchi Yamamoto, seen emerging from a Honolulu bomb shelter with their pet Mynah bird after an air raid drill in March 1942. The name of the commander in chief of the Japanese Fleet also happened to be Yamamoto, who would attack Midway Island in the western Hawaiian group three months later – making such names unpopular in the islands. Although many whites demanded the internment of these Orientals as security threats, the Islands' economy depended completely on them as the major work force. Even better, no act of sabotage was ever carried out during the war by Hawaii's Japanese population.

Scenes like this burning American oil tanker in Florida waters were not uncommon along the Atlantic seaboard during the first six months of the war. Hitler's U-boats clamped a blockade on the coast from Maine to the Gulf of Mexico as Allied escort ships and planes had to be diverted to the crucial transatlantic convoys to keep Britain and Russia in the war. The German submarines made the long crossing to the shallow waters of key coastal shipping routes, rested on the bottom by day, then fired on tankers and cargo ships which were silhouetted against brightly-lit seaport towns. When waiting for their nightly prey, German U-boat officers using binoculars could actually see residents through the windows of beach homes. The favorite locale for such attacks was off Cape Hatteras, North Carolina. During the spring of 1942, waterfront civil defense authorities finally clamped down and initiated dimouts and blackouts, which helped reduce successful sinkings. But oil slicks and bodies of merchant seamen still washed in from the sea.

AMERICA AT WAR 1942

Fear of a Japanese attack on the West coast caused the January 1, 1942 Rose Bowl football game between the University of Southern California and Duke University to be shifted from Pasadena, California to Duke's home field in Durham, North Carolina. Hatred of Japanese-Americans led to their evacuation from rendezvous points like the Rose Bowl to relocation centers in the interior. Here, in the predawn of March 24, a family piles its belongings onto its convertible at the stadium, one of 350 automobiles to carry 1,000 Issei and Nisei who formed a caravan, led by a motorcycle cop. Their destination was the camp at Manzanar, in California's barren Owens Valley, where others joined them by train. By this forced relocation, Caucasian racism reached its highest — or lowest — point in the deplorable search for scapegoats, crushing the civil liberties of over 100,000 American citizens.

Some of the Japanese-born Issei and American-born Nisei were sent as far east as Pueblo, Colorado, where they helped relieve the local farm labor shortage created by the draft and general migrations to the cities. The two Colorado farmers posing with their displaced onion pickers in October 1942 praised them as excellent farm workers – attested by these crates of onions and the plain fact that the Nisei saved the beet harvest not only in Colorado but Utah as well. But these Californians of Asiatic descent had lost nearly everything – homes, investments, businesses, even formal education – by being uprooted and moved.

"The young folks have lots of time for recreation," crowed captions of such innocuous scenes of the relocation camps as this one at Manzanar in May 1942. "And volleyball is one of the favorite sports for the Japanese interned at the Owens Valley Alien Reception Center." Such window-dressing masked the crude living conditions as suggested by the barrack buildings whose doors are left open to improve the circulation of air through the hot structures. But note the immaculate grounds on which the girls play – an admirable trait of Japanese people even in adversity. Also, being American citizens, the Nisei were hardly aliens. The stupid relocation policy was inflamed by the rabid Hearst press throughout the war, but cooler minds eventually saw its folly – notably Earl Warren, who as California's Attorney General had acquiesced in their removal and as Governor welcomed them back to their homes in 1945.

AMERICA AT WAR 1942

Nisei misfortunes could be converted to war uses, as when the Sumitomo Bank of San Francisco was turned over to the American Women's Voluntary Services (A.W.V.S.). Here, on April 12, 1942, two members of the two-year-old patriotic organization move office supplies into the former bank for use in recruiting female volunteers. Partly because of the spiffy uniforms of the A.W.V.S., it attracted movie actresses and upper class wives as well as more grass-roots gals. Also, like the Red Cross, but unlike other volunteer organizations, A.W.V.S. knew no racial or ethnic barriers to membership. Ironically, then, in this instance it exploited the plight of Asiatic-Americans.

Movie stars Bonita Granville and Jackie Cooper sell defense bonds and stamps to 600 members of the Los Angeles Federation of Sub-Deb Clubs, January 29, 1942. Granville's uniform is patterned after the Eagle Squadron, an all-American unit in the R.A.F. (Royal Air Force), she being an honorary captain in the Squadron. Both celebrities are about to depart for Washington, D.C. to attend the President's Birthday Ball.

Under the auspices of the U.S. Maritime Commission, the American merchant marine mushroomed after Pearl Harbor in a crash program of turning out cargo vessels and tankers faster than German U-boats could sink them. While the War Shipping Administration trained the crews, the Commission contracted older and newly-created shipyards to build the ships — especially Henry J. Kaiser's four yards in the San Francisco Bay area and two in the Pacific Northwest. Already standardizing freighters and oilers to last beyond the war years, Commission engineers designed and mass-produced a 10,500-deadweight-ton merchantman with a 9,100-ton cargo capacity just for the war, the Liberty ship — so ungainly that even maritime zealot FDR saw it as an "Ugly Duckling!" The first 60 went to the British, the rest were retained — over 2,700 Liberty and improved Victory ships. The standard T-2 tankers displaced 16,765 tons with a carrying capacity of 125,000 barrels of oil. American shipbuilders of merchant and warships in World War II had their finest hour (and final one, too, as the postwar industry would collapse), not only constructing but repairing ships. Well does this writer remember as a tyke seeing his father, Bill Reynolds, a shipyard electrician at Bethlehem Steel, staggering off a straight 24-hour repair job getting a vessel ready to return to sea from the docks of San Pedro in southern California.

The Japanese attack aroused fierce patriotism and a desire for revenge throughout America. One month after the disaster, these shipyard workers in the New York area volunteered to be transferred to Hawaii to help salvage and repair the sunken and damaged warships. Under the direction of the U.S. Navy's Bureau of Ships, several of whose officers are seen enlisting their cooperation on a wintry January day, these workmen and the Navy's mechanics and divers would restore all but a handful of the ships stricken by the Japanese on December 7. Many of those same restored vessels would even see combat in both oceans.

AMERICA AT WAR 1942

Though reluctant before Pearl Harbor to divert manufacturing resources away from aircraft to airships, the Navy changed its mind for cheaply – and quickly – produced "blimps," at the same time absorbing Goodyear's fleet of advertising nonrigids into wartime service. The squadron of Navy blimps in this huge hangar at Naval Air Station Lakehurst, New Jersey in January 1942 includes training blimps and the larger variety for coastal patrol. Each of the latter carried a machine gun and depth bombs, but their real value was in cruising no faster than 60 miles an hour over harbor approaches and above coastal convoys to spot enemy subs. While loitering over a U-boat, the blimp prevented the sub from surfacing to recharge its batteries – a fatal situation because after several hours poisonous battery gases would escape to asphyxiate the crew. Meanwhile, the blimp crew radioed for patrol-bombers to come and attack the sub.

By June 1942, these aircraft workers toiled in shifts at the final assembly hangar of Lockheed Aircraft's Burbank, California plant, operating round the clock to deliver P-38 Lightning interceptors for the Army Air Forces. Armed with a 20mm or 37mm cannon in the nose and four machine guns in the wings, this single-seat twin-fuselage fighter was powered by two Allison liquid-cooled engines. The unique design enabled the plane to fly at "lightning" speeds in excess of 400 miles per hour – one of the fastest planes of the war.

While the silk and synthetic stocking industries retooled to manufacture parachutes, careful hands had to "rig" the chutes – folding them into parachute bags. Two WAACs (Women's Auxiliary Army Corps) at Scott Field in southern Illinois are seen rigging chutes for the Army Air Forces Technical Command during the spring of 1942. This task had to be performed with perfection, for ensuring the chute opened correctly was a matter of life and death.

The Ford automotive plant complex adapted easily to the production of tanks, employing new techniques of manufacturing non-buckling steel armor plate, increased accessibility of vital parts, and simpler designs. Using equipment and material manufactured almost wholly at Ford plants, these assembly line mechanics put the final touches to M-4 Sherman tanks in November 1942.

Begun in September 1941, the Pentagon, on the Arlington side of the Potomac River opposite Washington, was the largest office building in the world. It was rushed to completion in one year, although its 35,000 War Department employees began moving in before the work ended. Two underground tunnels – one for buses, the other for private autos – provided easy access for Pentagon workers, some of whom are seen waiting to fill an empty late-morning bus two days before Christmas 1942.

This seemingly uncluttered and routine 1942 office scene at the New York headquarters of International Business Machines cloaks a major revolution in the history of modern technology – the introduction of the first fully automatic computer. Its construction was begun five years earlier by Harvard's Professor Howard Aiken and I.B.M. engineers – the Harvard Mark I, or Automatic Sequence Controlled Calculator. It used punched paper cards from these typists to enter numbers in 23 decimal digits to add, subtract, multiply, divide, and establish statistical tables, each calculation made in a third of a second. The electromechanical machine, located in another room, stood eight feet high and 50 feet long, with more than 3,000,000 electrical connections for wires totaling 500 miles!

AMERICA AT WAR 1942

"Greetings. You are hereby instructed to report for induction into the armed forces of the United States...." Such was the culmination of the selection process begun when Secretary of War Henry L. Stimson had drawn the first blue capsule from this giant fishbowl in October 1940. Inside each of 9,000 capsules was a slip containing a serial number used by local draft boards; a number had been assigned to each of the 16,316,908 young men who had registered after passage of the Selective Service Act in September. The bowl was the very same one used in 1917 for World War I. Brigadier General Lewis B. Hershey, director of the Selective Service Administration, ceremoniously allows an 18-year-old Navy enlistee, Seaman 2nd Class Albert Carter, to draw the last capsule on March 18, 1942, ending the lottery aspect of the initial draft. After registration, each man had to pass physical and mental examinations before being inducted into the Army (or the Navy, later in the war).

Newly-recruited Army nurses march – or rather walk – into wartime service, smiling at their steel helmets with netting for camouflage, ammunition belts, and assorted military equipment. The Army Nurse Corps, which dated from 1901, was enlarged for wartime service by turning to the American Red Cross for a pool of available reserve nurses. Some 40,000 responded before Pearl Harbor and eventually 60,000 in all, many coming from the federally-funded Cadet Nurse Corps. The Navy Nurse Corps, established in 1908, ultimately enrolled 14,000 women.

The popular Colonel Oveta Culp Hobby (inset, facing page), director of the W.A.C. (Women's Army Corps, after "Auxiliary" was dropped in 1943), greets some of her charges at a party in Washington. After the passage of the so-called "Petticoat Army Act" establishing the Corps, the 37-year-old Army public relations official, socialite, mother of two, and wife of a former Texas governor took over and convinced her superiors to allow a Lord and Taylor designer create the uniform. Wanting only mature women, the War Department set the minimum age at 20 for enlistees, although they averaged 25, and only 15 percent of them were married. In spite of a whispering campaign by critics that women enlistees were sexually promiscuous, the W.A.C. discharged lesbians and, until 1944, pregnant women as well. When several Wacs proved successful as antiaircraft gunners in the Washington area late in 1942, the Army asked for more to be assigned similar combat roles – whereupon the government cracked down and confined women to the administrative duties originally intended. Women in the Navy (WAVES), Coast Guard (SPARS), and Marine Corps provided an equally vital role by filling jobs which relieved thousands of men for combat overseas.

AMERICA AT WAR 1942

Soldiers and sailors wait for Washington, D.C.'s Stage Door Canteen to open on October 5, 1942, its second day of operation. Here they could dance with wholesome hostesses, enjoy live entertainment, and generally relax during off hours.

New York's Stage Door Canteen had the added treat for servicemen of rubbing elbows and being served meals and entertainment by the cream of Broadway's stars – and the not-so-famous, like radio singer Anita Kert, seen on stage in October 1942. The expressions of the lonesome guys on the floor and standing speak volumes about the importance of these canteens in keeping up the men's morale.

Washington's Stage Door Canteen had celebrities of a different sort waiting tables – political and economic leaders. Thus these sailors and soldiers (facing page) are greeted at the October 1942 opening night by the man responsible for giving them the tools with which to fight – Donald M. Nelson, director of the War Production Board. A low-key, affable man, Nelson was caught in the unenviable position of trying to balance the desires and needs of the industrialists, the military, and the rationing program.

"A good-lookin' gal" is part of the breakfast served up for these GIs at the Hollywood Canteen in August 1942. Her name was Peggy Digging, and she was an aspiring young actress. Although she never achieved stardom, she did her bit for the war effort by raising morale.

Wartime America was one great party for civilians and military folk with extra change and a great desire to spend it. One such festivity came to grief on a Saturday night in Boston on November 28, 1942. With over 800 people, including fans from the Boston College-Holy Cross football game, jammed into the popular Cocoanut Grove club, a carelessly handled match ignited the crepe paper decorations, creating a veritable fire storm. In all, 484 people perished in the country's worst civilian disaster, and others were left with disfiguring scars.

AMERICA AT WAR 1942

Typical of families throughout America, this Provincetown, Massachusetts fisherman and his wife and children remained tuned into the world on their radio. The news emanated from distinguished reporters like Gabriel Heatter ("Ah, yes, there's good news tonight...."), William L. Shirer, and Raymond Gram Swing; the laughs from Duffy's Tavern, George Burns and Gracie Allen, and Fanny Brice; suspense from *The Shadow*, *Jack Armstrong*, and *The Lone Ranger*; and quiz answers from *Information Please*, the *Quiz Kids*, *Truth or Consequences*, and bandleader *Kay Kyser's Kollege of Musical Knowledge*. Bing Crosby's *Kraft Music Hall* was a perennial favorite, while Walter Winchell's opening commentary "Good evening, Mr. and Mrs. America and all the ships at sea...." and Jimmy Durante's signoff "Good night, Mrs. Calabash, wherever you are!" are poignant reminders of the great days of radio. The medium demanded only one thing – imagination – which enabled the mental images of the listener to soar.

AMERICA AT WAR 1942

This San Francisco magazine rack in mid-1942 reveals the casual reading habits of wartime Americans. Behind the newspaper headlining German Field Marshal Erwin Rommel's advance toward defeat at El Alamein are *Life* for its pictures and news stories, and the fiction-and-fact favorites *The Saturday Evening Post*, *Colliers*, and *Liberty*. Conspicuous by their absence are *Time*, *Newsweek*, and *Harper's*, which quickly sold out due to paper shortages and had to be passed around. Short stories usually had a wartime setting. The pulp comic books centered on combat fantasies, cowboy and detective adventures, sports, and – in the lower right – the slowly-emerging genre of science fiction.

Man's best friend of the era was epitomized by the President's beloved Scottie "Fala" – posing outside the White House on his April 7, 1942 birthday with photographers, who seem to be posing for him! FDR made great hay following an August 1944 trip to the Pacific after a rumor circulated by the Republican opposition claimed that Fala had been left behind on an Aleutian island and that Roosevelt had sent a destroyer all the way back to pick him up. Reported FDR over the radio about Fala's reaction to the story: "His Scotch soul was furious!" Loved by many and hated by many others, FDR knew how to make Americans laugh in spite of themselves.

AMERICA AT WAR 1942

The war did not deter Hollywood's glitter and gossip, as when handsome British transplant Cary Grant married Woolworth heiress Barbara Hutton in July 1942. At the time, the newlyweds were learning Spanish from a count who, unknown to them, was a pro-Nazi agent whose spying activities were not uncovered for another year. Late in 1943 the Spaniard was convicted and jailed, just as Grant and Hutton began their separation which culminated in divorce.

A feisty, exuberant America was portrayed in one 1942 film, *Yankee Doodle Dandy*, and in two men therein – James Cagney portraying George M. Cohan. The brilliant song and dance by Cagney restored songwriter Cohan's music to patriotic preeminence. For Cohan, who died that year, had written "Over There" during World War I, not to mention even earlier favorites "Yankee Doodle Boy," "You're a Grand Old Flag," and "Give My Regards to Broadway."

The war film that endures as much for its cast and acting as for its patriotic message is *Casablanca*, released in 1942. Set in French North Africa, the story line was as involved as the status of France in those confusing years. After the fall of France in mid-1940, the Germans occupied only half of the country and depended upon a puppet French government in Vichy to run the rest of France and French Morocco and Algeria. The Free French who had escaped the Nazi conquest fought on as Allied spies and saboteurs in the Underground – represented in the film by Paul Henreid (in the background), married to Ingrid Bergman (right). Cynical American-born Casablanca nightclub owner Humphrey Bogart (between Bergman and Henreid) finally opts to help Bergman and eventually wins over the Vichy French police chief Claude Rains (second from left).

During late 1941 and 1942 American citizens responded enthusiastically to the government's call to give up all excess aluminum and tin to the war effort, as in this July 1941 collection outside the *New York Daily Mirror's* Aluminum Ball, where the crowd had come to donate and to dance. In spite of such patriotic zeal, Mayor LaGuardia could not offer junk dealers enough money to cart the stuff away, nor was this type of aluminum useful for weapons manufacture when melted down. The longer that such heaps of scrap lay idle, the more cynical people became about early rationing.

Except for the paraplegic FDR and the national fight against polio, the physically handicapped people of America had been generally neglected until World War II. But they pitched in from the beginning with "old braces to beat the Axis" as the original caption said of this scene on New York's West 57th Street. The discarded braces and crutches are added to old tricycles as part of the overall five-and-a-half-ton scrap drive. The heavy demands for manpower opened many doors of wartime employment for the handicapped, whose numbers also swelled with the return home of permanently maimed veterans looking for work.

AMERICA AT WAR 1942

This 1943 zootsuit was being transformed from a lower class teenage fad to a badge for street gangs and juvenile delinquents in urban ghettos. "A zoot suit – with a neat pleat – with a drape shape – with a stiff cuff" is how the 1940 song "A Zoot Suit" summed up the style in the jive talk of hip "cats." (The word "hip" was considered too square by those who were really "hip." A "cat" was any cool dude.) Anyway, from top to bottom, the suit usually included a wide-brim straw hat, padded shoulders, amply draped jacket to the knees, baggy pleated trousers above the waist as high as the chest and with tapered cuffs – all in dazzling contrasting colors and decorated with an extra long gold watch chain. Girl zoots donned an equally outlandish "juke jacket." A simple revolt against conventional fashion, the male zoot became a social rebel amidst wartime tensions and added a switchblade to his attire. To deter violent street gangs, Los Angeles outlawed zoot suits. Not without reason did Navy men in 1944-45 nickname Japanese kamikaze planes "zootsuiters" – desperate, suicidal assailants.

Leon Henderson's Office of Price Administration (OPA) in September 1942 declared zootsuits like this one to be downright unpatriotic because they wasted fabrics needed for the war effort (an assumption never actually proved). So bandleader Lionel Hampton uses chalk to mark the level to which trumpet player Karl George must shorten his jacket. Harlem jazz musicians who "grooved" at the Apollo Theater, Savoy Ballroom, and Minton's Playhouse – the "birthplace of bop" – had considered themselves as "sharpies" in such attire until the new word came along. Band members of the reed section curiously watch the proceedings, while the trombone and other trumpet men smile behind their "fan hats," devices used for muting and "ooo-wah" effects. "The Hamp" had a hard-driving orchestra typical of the war years, he himself a powerhouse of happy swing on the vibraphone, drums, and piano – on which he played rapid-fire numbers using only two fingers!

Waste paper remained a valuable commodity for recycling throughout the war. School children like these at St. Monica's Catholic school in New York brought collected newspapers to class on appointed days. This scene is May 24, 1944, with the kids at their desks savoring the approval of the nun who is their teacher. By then, the home front was on the offensive, and the children no longer had to dive under their desks in air raid drills.

Rationing sometimes took on absurd proportions, even in the military. For instance, to conserve the rubber, gasoline, and oil consumed by autos, Army airmen at McClellan Field in Sacramento, California rode bicycles around the base whenever possible. Even the base commanding officer, Colonel John M. Clark (left) returns the salute of Private First Class Lewis Hites.

The critical shortage of rubber led these New York showgirls from the musical *Sons O' Fun* to respond to the President's call for rationing in June 1942 by contributing their rubber garters and girdles! It wouldn't matter if their nylon stockings slipped down because these too were on the way out.

Before the war women clothed their legs with silk or lisle (cotton-thread) stockings, although the latter tended to bunch up around the ankles. The DuPont company developed a new fiber called nylon from the prewar plastics revolution except that it tended to wrinkle at the knees. DuPont eliminated these bumps in short order and on May 15, 1940 placed nylons on the counters for throngs of approving female customers. Nylons felt good and looked good, but there were never enough of them—especially after silk stockings began to be rationed in August 1940, followed by silk slips and panties, the material needed for parachutes. Finally, in 1942, nylon joined silk as a war industry, and that November women were enjoined to donate their older silk and nylon stockings to the war effort. In one week, the Vassar Club of New York collected one mile of the prized hose, a portion of which is seen here, for the American Women's Volunteer Service.

AMERICA AT WAR 1942

As nylons disappeared, women desperate to add color to their legs resorted to spray-painting their gams. So these two winsome workers at the Douglas Aircraft plant in Santa Monica, California, have their "stockings" sprayed on by an airplane painter during their lunch hour, July 1, 1943. Some women even had seams drawn down their calves using eyebrow pencils. These dimpled gals, surely not assembly line mechanics, display the fashionable casual look of the day: flowered hair, blouse and knee-length skirt or print dress, two-inch heels – and "stockings." The only distinctive adult male wartime styling is also evident here – a thin mustache.

Hoarding, having the right "connections," and outright theft led to a thriving business in "black market" goods – especially nylons. When police raided and seized storehouses of such precious ill-gotten commodities, the only fair, yet utilitarian way to disperse such contraband was to place them on sale to the general consumer. On June 24, 1944 these Southern women patiently wait in line at Greensboro, North Carolina to buy nylons seized from the black market. While one lady uses the time to read a book, leaning against a rest room door, another of middle age – obviously feeling out of place – casts a furtive glance at the joking gals of the younger set; one can only guess her thoughts. A fashion distinction between female age groups was headware – hats for the more mature, flowers for the youthful.

1943

Americans ate better than people of any other country in the world during the war, but rationing forced them to budget and economize – and even lose a bit of weight if they had it to lose. Orange juice in this well-stocked market is restricted to one can per person, but how many stamps were needed to be able to purchase one of those huge tins of kosher honey? With the shortage of sugar, honey became a major sweetening substitute. Dried vegetables and nuts were plentiful, and how about those "onions without tears?"

1943

AMERICA AT WAR

So rapidly and thoroughly had the nation tooled up for massive war production that by the spring of 1943 the growing weight of post-1940 industrial output enabled the United States to launch or support offensives on all the war fronts of the world. The new armies, fleets, and air forces which launched these attacks required such vast quantities of food and hardware that rationing had to be tightened on the home front. Defense plants, expanding to keep the machines of war flowing, employed unprecedented numbers of women as well as men. The country became more international in its outlook, rallying to supply ever more materials and foodstuffs to Russia and Britain for the defeat of Germany, and to China struggling against Japan. The economic boom increased profits and with them workers' strikes to insure commensurate wages. Army and Navy training camps dotted the 48 states, turning America into a vast armed camp.

American industry supplied the Soviet army which captured the entire German army before Stalingrad in January 1943 and which then began the slow but steady counterattack on the Eastern front. American and British strategic bombers systematically pounded German industries and cities in the face of the *Luftwaffe*. In North Africa, General Dwight D. Eisenhower's American armies drove eastward in a pincers movement which joined with Montgomery's British army moving westward from Egypt to force the capitulation of the entire Axis army. Anglo-American landings in Sicily and Italy during the summer convinced the Italians to expel Mussolini and join the Allies. In the China-Burma-India theater, Allied forces pressed into Burma and airlifted supplies over the Himalayas to the beleaguered Chinese, while in the Pacific our forces initiated a three-pronged offensive toward Japan: Admiral William F. Halsey, Jr. up the Solomon Islands, General Douglas MacArthur across New Guinea, and Admiral Chester W. Nimitz into the Gilbert and Aleutian islands.

The confidence which attended these victories was reflected in Irving Berlin's epic movie *This is the Army* and in the Fred Astaire vehicle *The Sky's the Limit* as well as in *We've Never Been Licked*, a cadet training drama filmed at Texas A & M College and using its fight songs. All-star movies like *Stage Door Canteen*, *Thousands Cheer*, and *Reveille with Beverly* combined the military and music. All-black casts and jazz groups enjoyed great success in the films *Cabin in the Sky* and *Stormy Weather* – both featuring singer Lena Horne and the latter movie including the last appearance of premier jazz pianist and vocalist Fats Waller, who died that year. On Broadway, Oscar Hammerstein II adopted Bizet's opera *Carmen* to the All-Negro musical *Carmen Jones* for 502 performances, and Ogden Nash and S. J. Perelman wrote the book and Kurt Weill the music for *One Touch of Venus* – 567 performances. But Richard Rodgers and Oscar Hammerstein topped them all with a run of 2,212 shows of *Oklahoma!* starring Alfred Drake. And in spite of a recording ban, people sang such new songs of love, war, and family as "Besame Mucho," "Comin' in on a Wing and a Prayer," and "I'll Be Home for Christmas."

AMERICA AT WAR 1943

By 1943 the American people were on the move – between Washington, D.C.'s Union Station, factories, military installations, and embarkation depots for the overseas offensives just starting to accelerate. This March 1943 scene of the capital's majestic train depot is dominated by the suspended poster depicting the nation's military heritage of fighting for freedom. The war years marked the end of a century of predominant American passenger travel by rail as postwar commercial aviation would take over, leaving the trains primarily to transport freight.

In common cause with their allies, the American government and people overlooked ideological differences with communist Russia in the desire to defeat Hitler. To back the Third War Loan Drive, Soviet Premier Joseph Stalin sent a message to Americans urging them to buy bonds which would enable the U.S. to continue the production of weapons for the Red Army then pushing back the *Wehrmacht*. Treasury Secretary Morgenthau shakes hands with Major General A.I. Belyaev of the Soviet Air Force after the latter has read aloud Stalin's message, September 22, 1943. The setting is a military exhibition near federal office buildings in Washington which includes a heavy cannon and, in the background, a U.S. Army band. Though capitalist Morgenthau and the Red general wear formal smiles, the immediate spectators appear skeptical about the foreigner — a survivor of dictator Stalin's bloody purges of perhaps 20 million Russians only five or six years before.

AMERICA AT WAR 1943

The voice of China was Madame Chiang Kai-shek, wife of the generalissimo who headed the Nationalist Chinese government. A lady of great intelligence and charm, she is helped on with her coat by New York Governor Thomas E. Dewey (left) and philanthropist John D. Rockefeller, Jr. after addressing 20,000 specially-invited guests at Madison Square Garden, March 2, 1943. Madame Chiang was the most visible symbol for Americans of the nation for whom the United States had gone to war in the first place. An articulate speaker, on this occasion she urged magnanimity toward the vanquished once the war was won. Ironically, the Chinese political scene was more complex than the average American realized, with Chiang Kai-shek the head of a corrupt government that worried more about the Chinese Communists than the Japanese invader. He himself would be driven from the mainland by these same Communists four years after the war.

Facing page: Madame Chiang takes tea – or is it American coffee? – in her suite at the Palace Hotel in San Francisco on April 1, 1943. She is receiving Lieutenant and Mrs. John A. Roosevelt during her five-day visit to the city. Roosevelt, youngest of the President's five children, was a Navy Supply Corps officer. One year later, while Chiang Kai-shek's armies reeled before a massive Japanese offensive on the continent of Asia, John Roosevelt was supply officer on the staff of Rear Admiral J.J. "Jocko" Clark aboard the new aircraft carrier *Hornet* – part of the Pacific Fleet pushing westward toward Japan. Of the other Roosevelt sons, Marine Lieutenant Colonel James was part of Carlson's Raiders' 1942 commando strike on Makin atoll; A.A.F. Lieutenant Colonel Elliott fought in North Africa; and Lieutenant Commander Frank, Jr., commanded a destroyer escort in Pacific battles.

AMERICA AT WAR 1943

Benito Mussolini's Italy became an enemy when it joined Hitler in declaring war on the United States in December 1941, and all 600,000 Italians living in this country though not yet naturalized were required to register as aliens. This indignity was felt equally by the 4 million Italian-Americans who were already citizens but generally pro-fascist before December 7. Immigrants or the offspring of immigrants, they had known so much resentment from native Americans that they had clustered in their own communities and often found refuge with the transplanted Sicilian Mafia crime syndicate. Very soon, however, they were boasting their loyalty and Americanism; after all, one young Joe DiMaggio had hit safely in a record 56 consecutive games for the 1941 New York Yankees. So they were immensely pleased when Italy kicked out Mussolini and went over the Allied side on September 10, 1943 — as heralded on this date by a barber in the Italian district of New York's Harlem. His patriotic window display includes a blue star flag denoting a son in service and a tally of 36 boys in uniform from the 111th Street neighborhood. General Douglas MacArthur is portrayed within the V-for-Victory.

An impromptu funeral in Harlem's "Little Italy" on September 10 celebrates the death of fascism in the motherland, with kids carrying the coffin, adults ceremoniously sweeping the way. FDR lifted the alien designation for unnaturalized Italian-Americans and smoothed the path for their obtaining a speedier citizenship. Although Hitler's armies still held onto much of Italy, the Italian state was no longer an enemy but a friend. The fact that these southern Europeans were being amalgamated into the mainstream of American life was no better illustrated than by Mayor Fiorello LaGuardia himself – and by the new singing sensation Frank Sinatra.

Poland, Hitler's original victim, did not escape the Nazi yoke, although some of its citizens did – like these refugee children saying grace at a camp on the grounds of the Santa Anita Race Track in Arcadia, California, November 7, 1943. Explained the original caption: "They are part of the 300 children who with 427 elders are Polish refugees, wards of the Polish government-in-exile who are on their way to Mexico where they will make their home for the duration." As in the case of China, however, the war would not end the oppression of Poland, which would remain under the foot of Soviet Russia for the next four decades.

Allied military personnel came to America's shores to be trained to fight or on leave from their ships. In July 1943 a Norwegian sailor and airman line up behind a U.S. Navy "swabbie" and a Coast Guardman to buy war bonds and stamps from an American Woman Volunteer in New York City. They are visiting the "Big Apple" to enjoy entertainment at swank establishments like "The Famous Latin Quarter" across the street.

This International News Service (INS) September 21, 1943 photograph bore the title: "Fighting Along Two Fronts." It was captioned, "New York...These Coast Guardsmen believe in fighting the Axis with all kinds of weapons. There are guns that they know how to handle, and there are monies that they know how to spend – where they will do the most good. One hundred Coast Guardsmen are buying war stamps from Sara Blohm at the War Center at 50th Street, between 6th and 7th Avenues." The U.S. Coast Guard had been shifted from the Treasury Department to the U.S. Navy for the duration, its cutters steaming on ice patrol in the North Atlantic, its men handling landing boats at jungle beaches in the South Pacific.

AMERICA AT WAR 1943

Home Front Americans watched many a military parade, especially during a war loan drive. To help raise $13 billion in the Second War Loan Drive, the Army stages a parade through Manhattan on April 15, 1943. A truck pulls empty bomb cases, followed by M-3 medium tanks, an Army band, and troops. Between individuals digging deep and financial institutions like the Chemical Bank and Trust Company on the corner, Uncle Sam obtained the revenues with which to whip the Axis. On this very same day, the Navy commissioned its second new aircraft carrier since Pearl Harbor – at Norfolk, Virginia. Named *Yorktown* for the famous ship of that name sunk at the Battle of Midway, she soon attained her own renown as "The Fighting Lady" from the 1944 documentary film of that title.

University campuses became home for officer trainees in many specialized programs. In May 1943 the morning bus at Colgate University in Hamilton, New York, picks up a group of Civil Aeronautics Administration War Training Service cadets for transportation to the airfield five miles away. While these 80 students undergo familiarization in the cockpit, another 600 cadets of the Navy's V-5 program receive preflight instruction at Colgate. Upon completing both stages of this initial training, the fledglings were destined for intermediate and advanced flight training at naval air stations across the country, prior to being assigned to Navy squadrons. By the time they reached combat, each would have over 500 hours in the cockpit — superbly trained pilots able to take on Japanese flyers with only half those hours.

Hunter College in the Bronx provided the physical setting — and swimming pool — for women recruits in the WAVES (Women Accepted for Voluntary Emergency Service). Like male sailors, these WAVES were required to be able to swim at least 50 yards. Although American women were markedly less hawkish than the men about the war, many enlisted without hesitation. Commander Mildred McAfee left the presidency of Wellesley College to head the WAVES, which eventually recruited some 100,000 women to serve. Championed by Eleanor Roosevelt and Maine's Senator Margaret Chase Smith, the WAVES faced harsh criticism from doubters aplenty who said the acronym stood for "Women Are Very Essential – Sometimes."

Three WAVE ensigns receive a tour of the Lake Michigan shoreline from a Coast Guard enlisted man and their first cruise aboard a vessel of war, the Coast Guard cutter *Minoco*. Their talents proved so essential in Washington and at naval installations throughout the country that Congress finally, at the end of 1944, allowed them to serve at Pacific Fleet headquarters at Pearl Harbor as well as in South America, the Panama Canal Zone, the Caribbean, and Alaska. (Hawaii and Alaska would not be added as states to the 48 stars of Old Glory until long after the war). The sea service also included 23,000 women Marines, 13,000 Coast Guard SPARS, and a plethora of civilian Navy "Chauffeurettes" who replaced men drivers at Navy bases. Lake Michigan, incidentally, provided a training area for thousands of Navy pilots who qualified in carrier landings aboard two aircraft carriers converted from peacetime Great Lakes sidewheel paddleboat pleasure steamers.

Enlisted female Marines "practice the manly art of self-defense," said the caption of this 1943 entanglement at Camp Lejeune, New River, North Carolina. Although the Corps refused to recognize any Marine element by a gender-related special title – a Marine was a Marine – it still did not expect its women to engage in combat, this body English notwithstanding. The director of the women's component was Colonel Ruth Cheney Streeter, a qualified civilian pilot and civic worker who had come over from the first group of WAVES, as had Captain Dorothy C. Stratton, director of the SPARS.

AMERICA AT WAR 1943

The only way women could find their way into wartime service as pilots was by joining the WASPs – Women Airforce Service Pilots – or, more specifically, the WAFS – Women's Auxiliary Ferrying Squadron. Skilled in the cockpit, over 1,000 of these women were employed as civilians to fly aircraft from the factories to A.A.F. fields or on weather hops and general hum-drum flying tasks which released the men to get the glory jobs. Still, as these WASPs show, they were confident and proud of their work, which they tackled with their sleeves rolled up. Wedding rings show that not all of them were single. The WASPs were disbanded at the end of 1944, by which time the Army had trained an excess of male pilots.

AMERICA AT WAR 1943

The Territory of Alaska figured prominently in the early months of the war, when Japanese forces captured Attu and Kiska islands in the Aleutians chain. U.S. Army Engineers built the Alaska or "Alcan" Highway during 1942, connecting the territory with Seattle via several Canadian towns, a measure designed to strengthen the northwest approaches to the continent. The southernmost Alaskan base was at Ketchican, a satellite Coast Guard station to Sitka from 1942 to 1944. Since the Coast Guard had no medical corps of its own, it relied on Public Health Service physicians, like this one conducting examinations of young Eskimo and Caucasian children at Totem Village outside Ketchican.

Supervised by auto workers, over 200 soldiers learned to dismantle, repair, and reassemble tanks at the Chrysler Tank Arsenal in Detroit early in 1943. Such skills enabled them to service damaged tanks on the field of battle. On the first try, a crew of 12 of these Army mechanics assembled an entire tank using only hand tools in just eight days.

President Roosevelt inspects the Tank Repair School of the Army's Armored Forces at Fort Knox, Kentucky. Seated next to him is Kentucky Governor Keen Johnson and in the front seat Brigadier General Joseph A. Holly. After this April 30, 1943 visit, FDR returned to Washington to deal with the coal miners, who made good their threat to walk out on strike next day, endangering overall wartime production.

Unique in America and the world was this mass production line of blimps at the Goodyear Aircraft Corporation in Akron, Ohio. After completion, these streamlined control cars, or gondolas, passed through the big doors at the end of the line where they were attached to the oblong gas bags for completion as lighter-than-air blimps. Carried aloft by helium gas, the airships kept the coastline well patrolled for the duration.

AMERICA AT WAR 1943

A sentimental poster reminiscent of World War I propaganda artwork appeals for donations to the American Red Cross. The image of its motherhood for the boys overseas may have been a bit overblown, but it was not far off the mark. The Red Cross guaranteed mercy and succor in the midst of death and devastation.

Two striking coal miners at Avoca, Pennsylvania, in the heart of the anthracite soft coal region, listen on the big console radio to Roosevelt's speech urging them to return to work, May 3, 1943. Under the leadership of United Mine Workers boss John L. Lewis, they refused, whereupon FDR had the government seize the mines the next day. The dispute dragged on for eight months, infuriating the public, the government, and the miners, but Lewis won for his miners a handsome pay hike from $45.50 to $58.87 a week, as well as other concessions. These salt-of-the-earth men, with their hat lanterns and freshly-washed clothes, stand ready to return to the pits if given the word. As patriotic as any Americans, they honor two brothers in the Navy and Army. The blue star flag represents one child in uniform, displayed next to a crucifix of these devout Catholics. A gold star flag represented a son killed in action and was usually displayed, proudly, in a front window—suggesting the fate of one of the boys in the picture frames.

The Greatest Mother in the World

WAR FUND 1943

AMERICA AT WAR 1943

In desolate, faraway places where American servicemen fought, radio personality Arthur Godfrey once remarked, "a cigarette is a friend." America's love affair with this potentially lethal habit (lung cancer almost killed Godfrey later) reached its peak during the war, as suggested by this superimposed picture of a G.I. lighting up on a photo of a benefit stage show entitled "Smokes for Yanks." The *Chicago Herald-American* sponsored the lavish September 1943 patriotic event at the Chicago Stadium. Millions of cigarettes were collected as the price of admission and sent on to the troops, who used them also as barter in foreign lands and as stakes in card games. Movies and melodies extolled the weed as both romantic and manly, as in Phil Harris' hit tune "Smoke, Smoke, Smoke That Cigarette!" And the ad men made tobacco part of the workaday, play-by-night world: "Chesterfields – They Satisfy" and "I'd Walk a Mile for a Camel" and "L.S./M.F.T." ("Lucky Strike Means Fine Tobacco," or, as we kids used to say, "Loose Suspenders Mean Falling Trousers!"). The legacy of the "cig" as a device for group acceptance and social conformity among the insecure young survives to this day.

Don Dunphy calls the play-by-play of the 1943 World Series over the British Broadcasting Corporation hookup for transmission to American forces in England, North Africa, and Italy. Like Mom and apple pie, baseball reflected the heart and soul of America and its traditional values – even though many of the current greats like Ted Williams, Hank Greenberg, and Bob Feller were "on leave" with the armed forces. Dunphy is seen at Yankee Stadium during the first game, October 5, during which Spud Chandler pitched nine innings, Joe Gordon homered, and Frankie Crosetti, rookie Billy Johnson, and Bill Dickey made key hits to beat the St. Louis Cardinals, 4-2. Chandler also shut out the Cards in the fifth and final game to sew up the Series for the Bronx Bombers.

Coney Island never failed to attract soldiers and sailors on leave in New York, like these two Coast Guardsmen from the station at Manhattan Beach and their dates frolicking in the sand on a spring day in 1943. The attractions of the popular amusement complex can be seen in the background, along with local kids watching the proceedings.

Like all wars, this one created a large, heartbreaking population of wounded veterans – many of whom would recover from their physical and psychological injuries and many who would not. Christmas time was always excellent therapy, evoking memories of childhood joys, comforts, and dreams. And no toy fascinated American males more than electric trains. Thus these recuperating wounded men at Halloran General Hospital in New York's Staten Island concentrate on setting-up a large train set around the Christmas tree.

AMERICA AT WAR 1943

The great 21-day, 16-city, coast-to-coast Hollywood Bond Cavalcade culminates at the Glendale railway station near Los Angeles before hundreds of enthusiastic spectators, September 26, 1943. It had netted $1,079,568,819 in war bonds, an immense contribution to the war effort. Film stars and lesser lights wave to the photographers: (left to right, front row) Sully Mason, Muriel Goodspeed, Harpo Marx, Ruth Brady, Doris Merrick, Mickey Rooney, Rosemary LaPlanche, Margie Stewart, and Dian Pendleton; (back row) tour co-manager Kenneth Thomson, Julie Conway, Dorothy Merritt, James Cagney, Kathryn Grayson, Betty Hutton, Lucille Ball, Ish Kabibble (Merwyn Bogue), Greer Garson, Kay Kyser, pianist Jose Iturbi, Georgia Carroll (Mrs. Kay Kyser), Fred Astaire, and Judy Garland. Ish Kabibble and Mason were musicians in the Kyser orchestra.

Some entertainers kept up civilian morale at home, while others donned uniform to serve in combat. Two (or rather three) of Hollywood's wartime stars at this Army Air Forces appearance are ventriloquist Edgar Bergen and his dummy Charlie McCarthy (the uniformed one on the stool!), and Lieutenant James Stewart. Pilot and plane commander of an Eighth Air Force B-17 who later bombed German factories, Jimmy Stewart would earn the rank of colonel before the end of the war. Every American knew the name of Charlie McCarthy's wooden pal Mortimer Snerd, but not until the next generation would his real live "sister" – Candice Bergen – achieve acting fame.

A resurgent wartime appeal of things Latin American was due partly to "The Brazilian Bombshell," Carmen Miranda. On stage, film, and records, she captivated audiences after arriving in this country in 1939 as a dancing, singing, double-talking comedienne who was perennially bedecked in colorful South American attire, notably her "tutti-frutti" hats of artificial flowers and fruits. Miranda appeared in no fewer than eight movies between 1940 and 1944, including this one, *Weekend in Havana*.

AMERICA AT WAR 1943

The "Moonlight Serenader" Glenn Miller evoked more nostalgia and warm feelings in servicemen about home and loved ones than any other wartime entertainer, except perhaps Bing Crosby singing "White Christmas." Disbanding his immensely popular civilian band in September 1942, he was directly commissioned a captain in the Army Air Forces, in which he formed an orchestra of over 50 classical, popular, and swing musicians and singers. With arrangements mostly by Jerry Gray, and propelled by drummer Ray McKinley, this aggregation musically surpassed even his civilian dance orchestra. As part of the A.A.F's Training Command, the group trained at Yale University and in May 1943 initiated its own network radio program "I Sustain the Wings." Miller and the only girl in the show, Marjorie Ochs, go over the script during a rehearsal that June. Transferred to England one year later, the orchestra took the title American Band of the Allied Expeditionary Force (A.E.F.), and Miller was promoted to major. Sadly, Glenn disappeared on a flight over the English Channel on December 15, 1944 (the small plane probably iced up and crashed); the news shocked the American public when it was released on Christmas Eve. A mammoth tribute to Glenn Miller was staged at New York's Paramount Theater on June 5, 1945 by the motion picture industry as part of the Seventh War Loan Drive. Bandleaders from Count Basie to Fred Waring and comedian Milton Berle performed, and Miller civilian band alum Tex Beneke observed that his old boss was only "missing." But he was gone forever – though not the music, which still lingers on.

Singing movie star Deanna Durbin represented the girl-next-door image in the minds of homesick boys overseas. Here, she poses to eat an ice cream cone in coy defiance of the sign during the filming of *Christmas Holiday*, released in 1944.

AMERICA AT WAR 1943

Life in America's colleges went on more-or-less as before, except for the conspicuous absence of the normal complement of civilian men. Co-eds of Bryn Mawr College wear the Pennsylvania school's traditional white skirts to roll beribboned hoops across the campus as part of the annual May Day celebration in 1943. Unbeknownst to anyone, World War II for Americans was at its midpoint.

Horseracing remained a passion for many wartime fun-seekers, except when it was occasionally curtailed due to wartime contingencies. Here the top jockey of the era, Johnny Longden, sits astride "Count Fleet" after winning the 1943 Kentucky Derby.

"Ah, my Deer!" said the caption to this August 29, 1943 depiction of a pledge's initiation into the Crown and Lance fraternity at Hofstra College, on New York's Long Island. The old "blind date" gag is applied as the initiate holds the hand of a girl and expects a kiss from her. Perpetrator of the hoax is the frat man on the right, star guard of the Hofstra football team. But the majority of male collegiates in 1943 were in uniform, courtesy of Uncle Sam.

AMERICA AT WAR 1943

Women doubled as workers and decoration whenever publicity demanded it. Thus Ann MacDonald stands atop a newly-completed tank at the Richmond Tank Arsenal in northern California in July 1943. Every tank, armored car, and tank destroyer was presented with a small American flag as it left the Arsenal, in this case by Miss MacDonald (a woman was a "Miss" or a "Mrs." in those days). Like many news stories, photographs were also censored where security might be at stake; in this picture, the censor has blocked out some of the vehicle's exterior equipment.

"Rosie the Riveter" became the universal appellation for women war workers, evoking the very picture of defeminized transplants from the home like these Bethlehem Steel shipyard welders – who in fact were sometimes regarded as "Winnie the Welder." The darkened background betrays the time of day – or rather night: the "swing shift," which women were encouraged to work while their children slept at home, especially if their husbands worked day shifts. For safety's sake, hair had to be cut short, or at least covered by a bandanna.

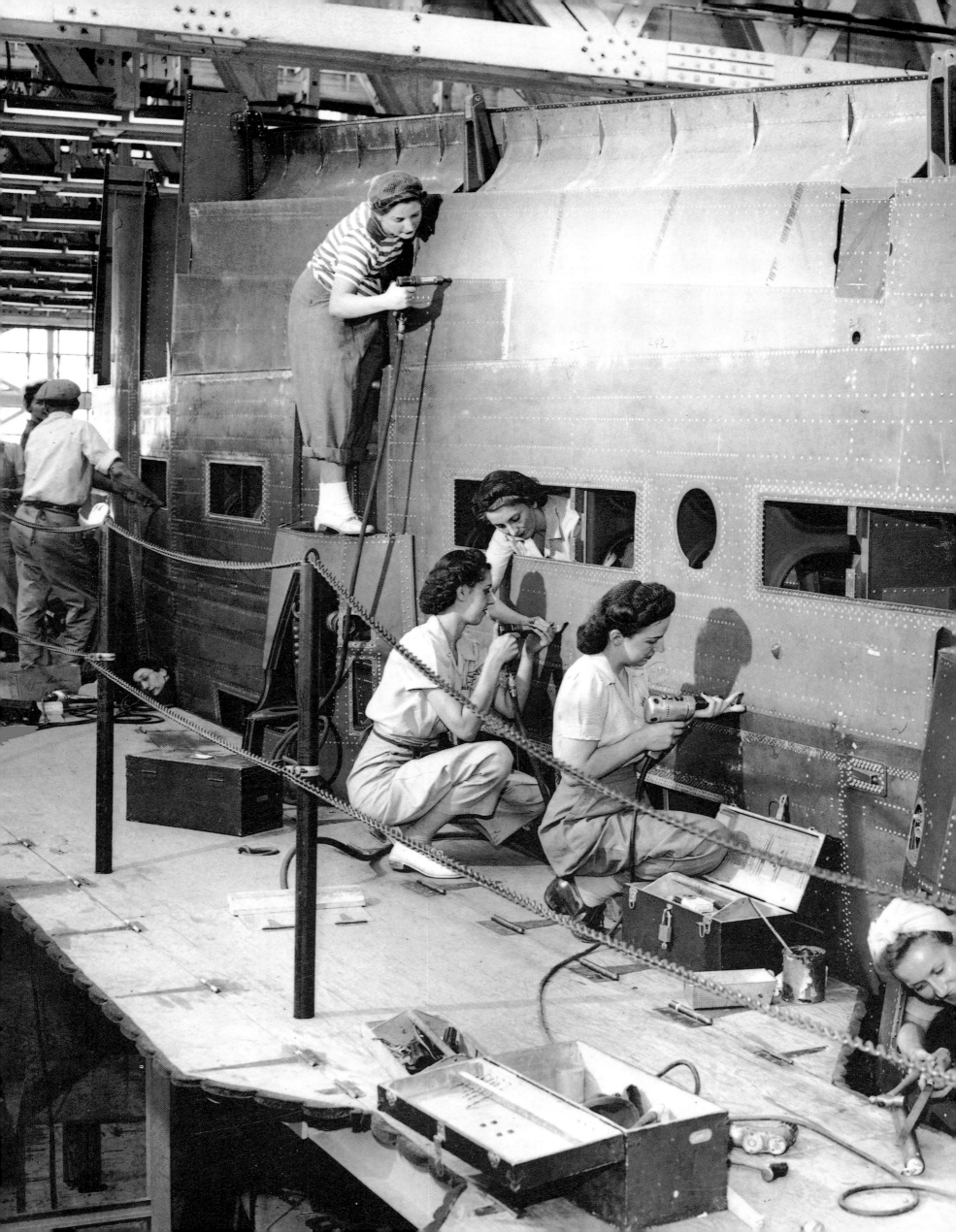

AMERICA AT WAR 1943

These "Rosies" do indeed rivet – on a gigantic wing section of a Douglas four-engined C-54 Skymaster cargo plane capable of carrying 15 tons of supplies or 50 combat-ready troops. This work is being done in the new Douglas plant in Chicago during July 1943. The still photograph fails to convey the fact that the rivet guns shook the "daylights" out of the holder. But Rosie rarely complained.

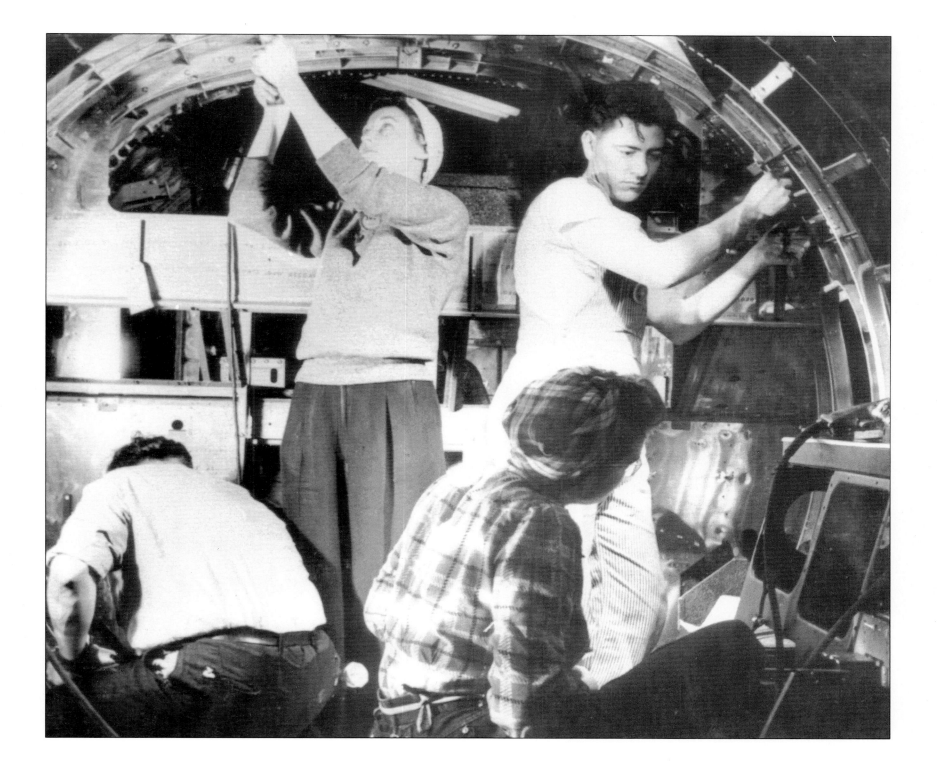

Men and women shared projects, like the interior of this B-17 Flying Fortress bomber, often with men harboring great jealousy toward the gals, even though the latter were generally paid lower wages. And husbands often objected to their wives working with men – for obvious reasons. Women had less physical stamina than the men – working with arms over the head is a good example – but they were less careless, had fewer accidents, and recovered more quickly from fatigue. Aircraft plants, however, used chemicals that caused more skin ailments to women and endangered pregnancies. Slacks became standard practical fashion, although safety shoes were usually oversized, or just unavailable.

Women were – and are – better suited than men, psychologically, emotionally, and physically, to perform meticulous, tedious, so-called "finger work" like sewing, typing, or assembling 37mm armor-piercing shells. At a large Midwestern aluminum factory converted to war production, these young gals do just that early in 1942, watched by men supervisors, getting these anti-tank projectiles ready for heat-treating. The inevitable tedium of the assembly line was eased by the good personal relations generally found in such plants.

AMERICA AT WAR 1943

Compared to shipyard Rosies, these women producing aviator's liferafts at a New England U.S. Rubber plant were fortunate indeed, for they were provided with a clean, well-lighted, roomy environment and were able to wear dresses and normally-styled hairdos. Yet, even these gals succumbed to the common pressures of women war workers, mostly the need to care for husband and children, which led to chronic absenteeism. If hubby was overseas, Momma was able to bring her baby to a child-care facility at the larger plants. Or she might quit her job for a time – like over the summer months when her school-aged children were at home and needed her.

While Rosie riveted metal wings together for combat aircraft, she also stretched and sewed fabric coverings over the light wings of training planes – which these women are doing at the Piper Aircraft Corporation plant in Lock Haven, Pennsylvania during February 1942. After the bare-ribbed skeletons were lowered onto the table, the fabric was affixed, then the finished product placed on the vertical rack to the right. The spotlight is necessary even in daytime because the window panes were painted black for maintaining nighttime blackouts while the swing shift worked. Long hair was safe on this assembly line.

AMERICA AT WAR 1943

Women were more sensitive to cleanliness than men – witness these two well-groomed assemblers of synthetic rubber assault gas mask carrier cases at the Firestone plant in Fall River, Massachusetts. If they could spruce up their rest rooms with greenery, curtains, and cots, their morale remained high. If the facilities were filthy, morale was low – and they would usually quit. Camaraderie between women was also important. The assembly process seen here replaced the old sewing together of canvas gas mask carriers. The worker on the left attaches fasteners and reinforcement patches; her co-worker assembles the entire case.

These Firestone workers at Fall River attach the oxygen canister to the gas mask for a final inspection. Firestone had developed these lighter weight masks for the Chemical Warfare Service, and the troops carried them ashore at Normandy in June 1944. But they proved useless, since Hitler never employed poison gas as the Allies had feared. The supervisor seen here is female, rare except in industries traditionally employing mostly women, such as textiles, because both men and women preferred male supervisors as being more effective foremen. Part of this bias was due to the lack of women supervisors' familiarity with the technology and pace of factory operations. They simply lacked the management skills and experience that only time could change.

This machinist's helper on the Pennsylvania Railroad in 1942 earned 42 cents an hour as she helped keep the trains moving. As a rule, women were honest and frank in admitting mistakes and proved to be ready learners in correcting them, and as the gentler sex they responded well to praise and constructive criticism. Male foremen who blasted them with the same blasphemous invectives used on men only wounded their sensitivities and thereby stifled performance. Since most women workers did not regard these jobs as permanent, they also cared less about employment security and benefits than did the men. They were interested more in such immediate matters as fatigue, overtime, and responsibilities at home.

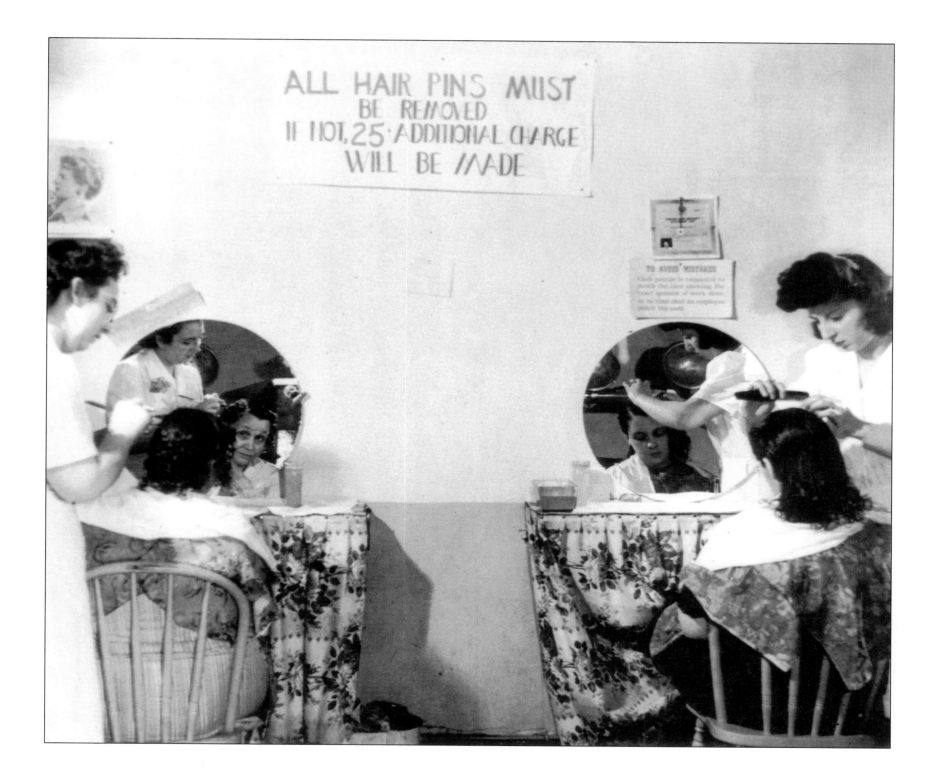

For the first time, factories had to offer social services for certain workers – the women that is. To keep up their spirits, hairdressers, like these at a plant in Buffalo, New York, were employed, and recreational facilities were added to counteract boredom in off hours. Counselors helped the women adjust, and health experts taught them exercises to relieve the soreness to certain muscles which they discovered for the first time. Menstrual cycles were thrown off by overwork, and pregnancies were often hidden for fear of losing jobs – only to have babies born right in the shop! These and a multitude of other concerns required attention by the companies, though lessons could only be learned as crises developed. But Rosie usually did what she was told – by her bosses and even by admonitions like this sign.

Is this Rosie for real? Her name is Madelene O'Leary, her employer the Bendix Marine Factory of Brooklyn, New York. The machinery is real enough, but she is absolutely gorgeous – her pressed new work suit looks brand new, makeup is perfect, fingernails are well manicured. Maybe it's her first day on the job. Dolls like her drew whistles from wolves and contributed to smashed fingers by distracted men. Yet, many gals sought out potential mates at the factories, and prostitutes found plenty of business until and unless they were caught by management. Whatever the problems over women in the work force, their contribution to the ultimate victory was immense.

AMERICA AT WAR 1943

Queing to obtain rationing books for purchasing commodities was a fact of wartime life, as on this 1943 New Orleans sidewalk scene. White, blacks, mommas and daddies with toddlers, and soldiers would all intermix in the shared practice of abiding by procedures laid down by the Office of Price Administration (OPA).

These women are registering for sugar ration books from local OPA administrators. All seem pleasant and inquisitive, save for baby, whose big yawn perhaps expresses their true feeling about the irritation of having to endure rationing at all.

When the OPA announced its decision to halt the sale of fish and canned meat beginning February 2, 1943, a mad rush by homemakers cleaned out stores of these items. The date for rationing fresh meat was fixed at March 29, triggering a run on meat "banks" like this pork retailer (facing page) of not-as-perishable smoked meats in New York five days ahead of the appointed date. When such stores were stripped of their stock, police often had to disperse the crowds.

This (left) was the store owner's view of the multitude making a run on his precious wares – in this case butter. With the OPA deadline set for banning the sale of butter at midnight on March 21, 1943, these consumers crowd into a grocery store on New York's Delancy Street that evening, but still see the humor in it for the photographer's benefit. Rationing followed several days later, and each individual's annual butter consumption dropped from 16 to 12 pounds. Artificially-colored oleomargarine took up the slack, despite a special tax on it that even Eleanor Roosevelt could not get rescinded because of the farm bloc in Congress.

"It seems like only yesterday that New Yorkers were concerned only with conga lines," the Latin American dance craze of a long serpentine of dancers with hands on the next person's waist. "Today," this caption observed, "the lowly spud is the prize for which these people patiently stand in line outside two special stores opened by Hearn's, of department store fame, at 149th St. and Third Avenue." Note that the people rushing to purchase the scarce "murphies" are mostly the elderly, who bring along their grandchildren while Mom and Dad work. Food shortages hit at different times and places in the country, and when Californians complained of a dearth of vegetables, they had only to be reminded that the relocated Japanese-Americans had been the ones who had raised and picked one third of the state's crops.

AMERICA AT WAR 1943

In April 1942, the OPA fixed maximum price ceilings – the General Maximum Price Regulation, or "General Max" – even before it initiated rationing. Happily, bananas stayed at their usual average price from March 1942, as seen at this Washington grocer's stand two months later. Clerk Joseph Wood seems pleased about it, as do his customers – Senator Harry S. Truman and his wife Bess. As Congressional watchdog over the government's conduct of the war, the Missouri Senator liked to see the fair regulation of all economic measures to assure victory. Vegetarians suffered least from the rationing, heavy drinkers perhaps the most. Ersatz whiskey, some of it downright lethal, was churned out by moonshiners and racketeers using talents honed during the Prohibition era of the 1920s.

AMERICA AT WAR 1943

AMERICA AT WAR 1943

Gas station owners were ordered to curtail hours of sales in order to discourage overconsumption as early as August 1941, and the "Victory" speed limit of 35 miles per hour helped as well. At four gallons per week, the auto owner with an "A" sticker could make 15 miles per gallon or go 60 miles a week around town, and pleasure driving was flatly outlawed by the OPA in January 1943. Car poolers carried "B" stickers to get to work; medical and other essential people used "C" for a larger allocation; "T" stood for truckers, with unlimited fuel, and "X" for Congressmen – no rationing at all, bringing on widespread criticism. As OPA introduced detailed rules and regulations over travel by car, enforcement became a burden, and the black market for gas and tires flourished.

A policeman checks a gas rationing booklet as a station wagon moves toward the head of the line at a filling station. The abridgment of unlimited travel by auto led to markedly reduced traffic, lower revenues from gasoline taxes, and fewer auto accidents and fatalities. The milkman could make his home deliveries every other day, since more Americans owned refrigerators than the antiquated ice boxes, and some newspapers resorted to using delivery wagons pulled by horses. Also, people tinkered more with their prewar vehicles, making the aging roadsters last for the duration until postwar auto production could resume.

1944

"Der Bingle" is the German-tinged nickname many wartime fans gave the immensely popular singer Bing Crosby, seen entertaining troops with Dinah Shore on a U.S.O. tour in France during October 1944. Known as a crooner during his salad days, Crosby had changed to a more relaxed, easy-going delivery by the 1940s. Young Dinah had already become a leading vocalist in 1941 on the radio, on records, and in films, doing much to raise the morale of American servicemen.

1944

AMERICA AT WAR

"Fortress America" delivered the goods of war so well that the economy was supplying and feeding the world – not only the Allies, but refugees and liberated countries as well. American farms enjoyed bumper crops to match industrial production, and rationing continued unabated. Such prosperity encouraged people to clamor for limited reconversion to domestic production. FDR made vague promises to provide postwar social benefits and pressed for a new international organization to insure the hard-won peace, but it was his inspired wartime leadership which assured his re-election to a fourth term in November 1944. Public demands aside, however, the military rejected any diversion of war production – and with good reason, for the fanatical enemy doggedly contested the several Allied offensives.

In the ETO, Allied landings were stymied by the Germans at Italy's Anzio beachhead early in the year, but the advance eventually pressed on to liberate Rome at mid-year. The great military event was D-Day – June 6, 1944 – when Eisenhower led the Allied invasion of Hitler's "Fortress Europe" at the Normandy beachhead on the French Atlantic coast, followed in August by another assault in the Mediterranean. The two prongs united to drive the Germans back to the Low Countries, where, however, they suddenly counterattacked at Christmastime in the epic Battle of the Bulge. But the greatest ground war occurred on the Eastern front, where the 5-million-man Red Army pressed into Germany from the east. In the Pacific, Nimitz's great fleet captured the Marshalls, Marianas, and Philippine Islands, supporting MacArthur's victorious armies in New Guinea and at Philippine Leyte and Luzon. In Asia, the Japanese overran most of Southeastern China, but the Allied completion of the Stilwell Road linked India and Burma with China, from which U.S. B-29 bombers began to operate as far as Japan – joined by more B-29s from the Marianans late in the year.

Broadway could "Follow the Girls," and Hollywood could "Follow the Boys" overseas as war music continued to dominate popular tastes. The men in uniform lamented military life with the "G.I. Jive," sent home the enemy's universally popular melody "Lili Marlene," and took a "Sentimental Journey" in remembering their loved ones: "I'll Be Seeing You" and "Goodnight, Wherever You Are." They itched for "Amor" (love) from the likes of movie starlets Esther Williams (in *Bathing Beauty*), Rita Hayworth (*Cover Girl*), and, as always, Betty Grable (*Pin-Up Girl*). Betty Hutton even wore a Navy uniform in *Here Comes the WAVES*, which exuded optimism with the hit Harold Arlen and Johnny Mercer number, "Ac-cent-tchu-ate the Positive." War workers coming off the all-night swing shift groaned, "Milkman, Keep Those Bottles Quiet," and man-hungry gals warned, "You Can't Ration Love," although the pickings were lean: "They're Either Too Young or Too Old." One tune, though, held up great hope: "I'm Beginning to See the Light" – Victory.

Camouflage remained a constant part of the landscape on both coasts, where Civil Defense officials never discounted the possibility of air raids. Indeed, Japan started development of a four-engine long-range bomber just for this purpose early in 1944, but had to give it up due to lack of war materials. Late in the year the Germans unleashed their V-2 rockets against London and were developing a multi-staged A-9/A-10 transatlantic rocket for use against New York when the war ended. Unmanned, however, the rocket would have rendered the camouflage superfluous. This peaceful-looking village near Seattle was in fact an elaborate chicken-wire townscape superimposed atop a Boeing aircraft plant building B-29 bombers with which to bomb Japan. The two women navigate across it by using a safe catwalk.

One oddity of World War II was the international position of the Soviet Union. In Europe, Russia was the arch enemy of Nazi Germany, while in the Pacific it was a neutral, having signed a nonaggression pact with Japan. A quarter of America's Lend-Lease aid to the U.S.S.R. went via the embattled North Atlantic, another fourth via the South Atlantic, Indian Ocean, and Persian Gulf through Iran. But fully one-half of U.S. aid to the Soviets went across the North Pacific, virtually unmolested by Japan. When a Russian oil tanker pulled into Los Angeles harbor early in 1944, the crew gave away a litter of its mascot's puppies to Bethlehem Steel shipyard workers, one of whom was the author's father, who brought home a two-month-old mutt on Valentine's Day. Teased mercilessly by the Reds, "Smokey" was mean and mangy for all 17 years of his life, but a loyal pet who remained a constant reminder to me of the war years until I went off to college. Here we are about the time the war ended.

THERE'S A PLACE FOR YOU IN THE NAVY Enlist Today

HELP HOLD "FULL SPEED AHEAD FOR VICTORY"

AMERICA AT WAR 1944

To release men from guard duty at South Weymouth Naval Air Station near Boston, the security police force decided to hire civil service women who could handle a riot gun. Their supervisor, seen instructing them on the mechanics of the weapon, is Marine Lieutenant Chester H. Knowles, who taught them to fire from the shoulder or from the hip. South Weymouth was home for six Navy blimps which patrolled the New England coast, and these ladies were also trained to operate antiaircraft guns. The warm ski-type attire was necessary in that month of February 1944.

"Dressed to Kill," punned the INS caption writers, these "Guardian Angels" are transported to their posts, riot guns at the ready. Note the security badge, with chain holding a police whistle. The open van was another reason for the functional suits during frigid New England winters. Odd, though, that servicewomen were forbidden from engaging in combat, while female civil servants were armed to the teeth.

World War II so unified the American people against the Axis that organized pacifism virtually disappeared, while the majority of Americans resented the pronouncements of peace advocates in the midst of the great struggle. The Nazi treatment of the Jews inflamed even the hard-line antiwar zealots. Still, individuals like retired 80-year-old Reverend Henry W. Pinkham of Newton, Massachusetts, carried on futile and isolated protests. He is seen picketing the annual meeting of the American Unitarian Association in Boston, May 25, 1944.

AMERICA AT WAR 1944

During 1944 the first large number of veterans returned home to be discharged, some missing one or more limbs. But wartime progress in prosthetics enabled most of these men to be fitted with artificial hands, arms, or legs and trained in their use by occupational therapists. Lieutenant Henry Bass of the Army's Signal Corps lost both hands in a dynamite explosion in February 1944, but by constant practice at Walter Reed General Hospital in Washington, D.C., he was soon able to handle a cigarette and write again, as seen here the following October.

The great strides in rehabilitating servicemen blinded during combat were proved in a Philadelphia crew race on the Schuylkill River between crews of both services who were blind. Winning captain of the Navy crew Robert Casterline (right), from the Philadelphia Naval Hospital, is congratulated by Army captain Vincent Trypuc, of Valley Forge General Hospital.

The famous ski-jump nose of comedian Bob Hope found its way into the hearts of fighting men and women in World War II (and several subsequent conflicts). He had just turned 42 when pictured in U.S.O. uniform chatting with three Navy radiomen in June 1945. By then, his theme song "Thanks for the Memory" had become an appropriate trademark for the war years, used on his radio show and in travels to entertain the troops. In these performances and several Road movies, he carried on an innocuous "feud" with Bing Crosby—all part of his well-timed wisecracks, aided and abetted by wide-eyed, mustachioed, and loud, one-note voiced screwball Jerry Colonna. And he sang with Frances Langford backed by Skinnay Ennis' orchestra. Thanks for the memories, Bob!

No more lavish spectacle greeted visitors to the "Big Apple" than the Radio City Music Hall. And the heart of its regular stageshow was 36 gorgeous gals — or rather 72 well-turned legs — known as the Rockettes. High stepping, they tap-danced in precision choreographed numbers, the sounds of their taps falling evenly on the ears of all 6,200 customers, thanks to the perfect acoustics of the place. Music from the 4,000 pipes of the giant Wurlitzer, the largest organ ever installed in any theater, consumed the audience, which marveled equally at the great arches sweeping above on the vaulted ceiling. The Hall epitomized the bigness of America—prewar, wartime, and postwar.

AMERICA AT WAR 1944

While the Allied Expeditionary Force stormed ashore at Normandy in early June 1944, home front revelers continued to dance up a storm of their own, as seen the same week at this "corner for the hepcats" located in Coney Island's Steeplechase Park. Said the caption: "Hot bands make with the boogie-woogie here while the boys and girls swing, sway, and chop up the rugs." By this point in the war, women's slacks had become ubiquitous, at least for daytime activities like this outdoor dance. And, look! Nylons on the gal in the sailor dress, probably purchased on the black market for a whopping $5 a pair. Or are they painted on, with a penciled "seam"?

AMERICA AT WAR 1944

"The Mussolini of Music," James Caesar Petrillo (center) fought for – and won – better pay and royalties for career music makers as president of the American Federation of Musicians. Already a power in his local Chicago union by the time he took over the A.F.M. in 1940, he called a recording ban by all musicians on August 1, 1942 until the record companies agreed to pay bandsmen royalties for the sale of records on which they performed, and for the use of those records over the radio. All the companies but Columbia and Victor caved in on September 18, 1943, but in the meantime singers, who did not belong to the union, had established themselves in the studios. Petrillo is seen with two of his lieutenants at a Chicago convention in October 1944, the month before the two recalcitrant record companies yielded. The big bands, already in decline from travel restraints, the draft, and changing popular tastes, never fully recovered.

The movie houses kept packing them in during 1944, at the phenomenal rate of 90 million customers a week! Music and comedy continued to be the set piece for war-weary workers and servicemen, but with a new twist from the starlet who swam her way onto the silver screen – Esther Williams. She is seen in the 1944 film entitled, not surprisingly, *Bathing Beauty*, with the "framed" Red Skelton providing the laughs.

AMERICA AT WAR 1944

The United States was totally unprepared for Frank Sinatra – or rather, for the teenagers' response to him. Physically the antithesis of the heroic figure one might expect in wartime, he was instead a scrawny, almost frail, but much admired vocalist with the Tommy Dorsey Orchestra in 1940-42. As such, his romantic songs alongside the Pied Pipers quartet (matched by Ray Eberle and the four Modernaires with Glenn Miller's band) reflected changing public tastes; even Dorsey took on the sobriquet "sentimental gentleman of swing." But when Sinatra appeared as a single in concert at New York's Paramount Theater in January 1943, the bobby-soxers went absolutely wild. Apparently in need of a symbol for their own generation, they rejected the older Bing Crosby and swooned over "Frankie's" soft, well-phrased hits like "You'll Never Know." His personal appearances caused riots – a theretofore unknown reaction to any American singer – as at Grand Central Station before he boarded the train for Hollywood in August 1943. 1944 found Sinatra singing on radio's *Your Hit Parade*, on numerous recordings, and in two movies. His wartime achievements were crowned in 1945 when he co-starred with dancer Gene Kelly in the hit movie musical *Anchors Aweigh*.

Inside the Paramount, the gals smile, applaud, bite their nails, skip heart beats, and – when each song ends – squeal, "Oh, Frankie!" Many older observers of the Sinatra phenomenon believed that he would have to get into some kind of uniform to sustain his popularity. But he never did, and by the time of this October 1944 concert he was approaching 29 and had a wife and two kids, making him exempt from the draft – and his fans never required him to go to war.

AMERICA AT WAR 1944

General Dwight D. Eisenhower – "Ike" – had become a well-known and friendly face in the newspapers of America by the time of this May 14, 1944 photograph. Taken in England, it shows him tired though alert as Supreme Commander of the A.E.F. planning the invasion of Hitler's Fortress Europe. Three weeks later, on June 6, his name was on the lips of all Americans, as his voice on network radio announced the D-Day landings at Normandy, France to begin the liberation of western Europe. The fact that he had already successfully freed North Africa, Sicily, and southern Italy from the Nazi yoke assured Americans' confidence in him. And succeed he would again, leading the Anglo-American drive into Germany to link up with the Red Army from the East. Postwar symbol of the Great Victory, Eisenhower was a natural choice for President in 1953.

Senator Harry Truman was not a natural choice for the Vice Presidential nomination on the Democratic ticket in 1944. Although a man of unquestioned integrity as Senate investigator of the national defense program, he did not command the public acclaim or FDR's preference for either incumbent Vice President Wallace or the so-called "Assistant President," James F. Byrnes, Director of War Mobilization. But Wallace had offended too many party regulars, and when FDR proposed Byrnes to Sidney Hillman, head of the C.I.O.'s Political Action Committee, the latter replied that neither organized labor nor Northern blacks would support the South Carolinian. Reluctant to split the party, Roosevelt accepted Truman as a compromise running mate. He beams in his office on August 4, 1944, shortly after receiving the nomination. After succeeding to the Presidency upon FDR's death the following April, HST appointed Byrnes Secretary of State.

Vice President Henry A. Wallace was the darling of the liberals during the war. His mid-war speech "Toward a Free World Victory" identified World War II as a major step in a global people's revolution, including Russia's, against imperialism, economic monopoly, and hunger – a clarion call for a reformed world order that respected columnist Raymond Clapper compared with Lincoln's Gettysburg Address. But Wallace's book, *The Century of the Common Man*, was criticized for its vagueness and platitudes. Still, he was FDR's clear choice to continue a second term in the Vice Presidency, for he represented the progressive ideals of the prewar New Deal. Most Democratic Party regulars wanted him and chanted "We Want Wallace" at the convention. And Wallace expected to be renominated. But too many Southerners opposed him as too liberal, and city bosses in an urbanized America had no use at all for the Iowan and former Secretary of Agriculture. FDR finally agreed to let Wallace go in favor of either Supreme Court Justice William O. Douglas or Senator Truman; the party manipulators chose the latter. Disappointed by his July 1944 convention defeat, Wallace did not begin campaigning for Roosevelt's re-election until this September 21 speech at a Madison Square Garden rally. He served as Secretary of Commerce in the Truman administration, but his sympathetic opinion of the Soviet Union generally fell on deaf ears in the postwar period.

The war bond drives continue unabated to support the liberation of France and the Low Countries. In July 1944 these sailors at Naval Air Station Whidbey Island, in Washington's Puget Sound, chip in by purchasing bonds from the officers at the table.

AMERICA AT WAR 1944

The assault on the continent spurred Allied leaders to accelerate planning for the postwar world. Representatives of the "Big Three" convened at Dumbarton Oaks in Georgetown, D.C., in August 1944 to draft the initial plan for the United Nations. Strolling through the gardens of the estate are, left to right, the chief delegates of the United Kingdom, Sir Alexander Cadogan; the U.S.A., Edward R. Stettinius, Jr.; and the U.S.S.R., Andrei A. Gromyko.

A peerless campaigner in his three previous elections to the High Office, Franklin Roosevelt did not disappoint the Party or the country in his fourth bid. On October 21, 1944 he braves a steady downpour in an open convertible to let the voters of New York's boroughs get a look at him in a four-hour, 50-mile-long motorcade. The electorate ignored his 62 years and questionable health to give him 432 electoral votes to rival Dewey's 99 on November 5. In fact, however, the President was just about worn out.

Among the many promises which tantlized a population clamoring for partial reconversion to a peacetime economy was television. Experiments since the mid-1920s had gone relatively unnoticed by the public until the New York World's Fair in 1939 had presented a TV set with a screen about 8 by 10 inches. No model was more impressive than this Admiral combination radio-phonograph-recorder-television set console being demonstrated by Admiral Company executives in Chicago in November 1944. The American people were more than ready for peace, but network TV would not become a reality until 1948.

AMERICA AT WAR 1944

The rural poor also did their part as a matter of survival as much as for helping the war effort. These Cherokee Indians and white Oklahoman children of the town of Cherokee man their hoes, which stand taller than them. Note how many of these kids lack shoes. The 4 million "Okies" and "Arkies" (from neighboring Arkansas) who had migrated to California during the depths of the Depression were little better off in the Golden State until farmers as well as factories needed them for wartime jobs.

Comely Chicago Victory gardener Katherine Tracey completes her scarecrow to keep away hungry birds during the 1943 planting season. That year 20½ million Victory gardens totaling four million acres produced a phenomenal eight million tons of food and one-third of all vegetables consumed by Americans. Homemakers took courses in nutrition and learned how to use the popular wartime pressure cookers in canning their vegetables and fruits. By 1944 one-fourth of the nation's city dwellers were tending 8-by-10-foot Victory gardens like Katherine's.

Enterprising Americans on farms and in the cities took a page from World War I by planting their own Victory gardens at the outbreak of war – even over the objections of a Department of Agriculture which initially thought them unnecessary and too amateurish. By April 1942, however, over six million Americans had them, forcing the USDA to take concerted action by providing professional advice. This acceptance of reality came none too soon, and as rationing began during the fall, Agriculture Secretary Claude Wickard called for 18 million Victory gardens both to enable Americans to save food coupon points and to release the usual harvests for consumption by the armed forces and Allied peoples. Agricultural Professor Harry Nelson of San Francisco Junior College instructs his daughter Pat (left) and two of her Girl Scout playmates to plant seedlings on a cloudy day or shaded by "paper tents."

Extra vegetables from early New Jersey Victory gardens in 1942 are collected and canned by members of the American Women's Volunteer Service of Long Branch, a summer resort area some 30 miles south of New York. Once the pressure-boiled foods are sealed in the canning jars, the jars are boxed for distribution to casualty stations to be stored for emergencies. The A.W.V.S. ladies wear very stylish work coveralls over their dresses. As homemakers grew new and greater quantities of vegetables, Americans' diets changed, with more salads, vitamins, and recipes than ever before – a fringe benefit of the war years that would survive. With two-thirds of all American backyards sporting a Victory garden, the USDA tried to raise the total number from 20-plus to 22 million during 1944, but the easing of rationing and waning enthusiasm led instead to a slight decline. Indeed, most families probably had sufficient canned goods in their pantries to tide them over for another year. And whatever happened to these stored emergency jars?

Mother Nature smiled on American farmers with ideal weather for crops during 1942. The bumper harvest created a crisis, however, because the draft had claimed too many farm laborers. Women' everywhere rushed into the breach to pick the ripened fruits and vegetables before they rotted – the A.W.V.S., the uniformed Women's Land Army organized just for this purpose, the YWCA (Young Women's Christian Association), the High School Victory Corps, and the Women's Ambulance Defense Corps. This Van Nuys, California unit of the W.A.D.C., directed by Captain Betty Yohalem (right), brings in the tomatoes from L.A.'s San Fernando Valley in late October 1942. The crops were rescued nearly everywhere, a not insignificant victory during a year of Allied military reverses.

AMERICA AT WAR 1944

An army always marches on its stomach, so the saying goes, but the U.S. Army put food production to another constructive use – helping the wounded convalesce by tending Victory gardens. These two combat veterans pick carrots in the Victory garden at Miami Beach under the general auspices of the A.A.F. Technical Training Command, which shared Florida's many military airfields with the Navy's Bureau of Aeronautics. The hospital that assigned these men to light farm work insisted that they only do it for short periods to prevent exhausting themselves. Eddie Roberge (left) hails from Iron Mountain, Michigan, and Dennis McInerney from Brooklyn, New York.

The good growing weather returned in 1943 and with it the same critical labor shortage in the fields. When the potato crop in the Virginia tidewater region could not be harvested, Governor Colgate W. Darden, Jr., called upon the most available source of manpower in the area and no stranger to spuds – the U.S. Navy. The Fifth Naval District at Norfolk responded with 500 sailors. On this June day, one "swab" drives a tractor which pulls the digger that unearths the tubers. Rows of seagoing men fill gunny sacks with the exposed potatoes, probably chuckling over the irony of doing the very chores they thought they had escaped by joining the sea service. Also, as sailors they knew something about peeling spuds – although potato-peeling machines were being introduced into the fleet. A local lad kneeling with his own basket takes in the spectacle. Three months later, Congress took steps to lessen future crises by deferring two million farm workers from the draft.

AMERICA AT WAR 1944

The Axis enemy delivered to the United States more than 130,000 farm workers in the form of prisoners of war. These German "PWs" have just alighted from farming trucks to return to their temporary barracks after a day of picking peanuts from fields in Dublin, Georgia, September 4, 1943. In Charleston, South Carolina, some 1,100 German and 400 Italian prisoners were engaged in farming and working in fertilizer plants and at the local paper mill. Their supervisors viewed the Italian switchover to the Allies that month of September with mixed blessings. The bosses were glad they no longer had to depend on the Italians, who tended to goof off on the job and were the worst workers ever encountered, unlike the industrious Germans. But now the Italians were to be employed as free aliens, helping to win the war and presumably with a better attitude. Wartime Charleston enjoyed its greatest prosperity since pre-Civil War days, especially because of its thriving Navy shipyard.

The plight of the American Negro and other disadvantaged minorities was a constant concern of the First Lady, Mrs. Eleanor Roosevelt. She is decorating Army Private Sam Morris, a prewar heavyweight Chicago boxer, for heroism in saving ten people from a Seattle meat packing plant when a bomber crashed into it. The month is April 1943. Secretary of War Stimson had little patience with Mrs. Roosevelt and her liberal "cherubs" like Vice President Wallace who wanted to advance civil rights while there was a war to be fought. But she persevered, on one occasion announcing with keen insight, "A wind is rising throughout the world of free men everywhere, and they will not be kept in bondage."

Stimson appointed a black judge, William H. Hastie, to handle ticklish race problems for the War Department. But the more that Hastie demanded integration of black with white units in training centers and combat operations, the more Stimson resisted, influenced by the strident traditional racism of the white South. Eleanor notwithstanding, FDR toed a careful line not to alienate either element of the Democratic electorate – white South or urban blacks – which led Hastie to resign in 1943 after two years of frustration. But no honest person could gainsay the clear truth that Negroes could die just as readily as Caucasians for the American flag – as evidenced by this black soldier cleaning his rifle on a troopship crossing the Atlantic to the British Isles in August 1942.

AMERICA AT WAR 1944

Heavyweight champion of the world Joe Louis served as an inspiration for all Negro Americans. "The Brown Bomber" entered the Army and lost no time in doing all he could to serve his country. With boxing gloves and shoes, he heads for training quarters at Fort Dix, New Jersey in early March 1942 to prepare for a bout for the benefit of the Army Emergency Fund. On that occasion, in Madison Square Garden, Louis made a memorable statement about the war: "We're going to do our part, and we'll win 'cause we're on God's side." Son of an Alabama sharecropper, he displayed a quiet sportsmanship throughout the war and endured the indignities heaped upon his race with deep religious conviction.

Of all the services, the U.S. Marine Corps most resisted the employment of blacks, and when it enlisted them, like all the services, it confined them to labor and support assignments like the 51st Composite Battalion, seen on inspection at Camp Lejeune in March 1942.

"The 'Singing Engineers' Can Dance, Too," announced the caption for this March 1942 photograph from the Army base at Fort Bragg, North Carolina. "They call the 41st Engineers the 'Singing Engineers' but the boys are proving that they can dance as well. Another thing they're pretty good at is building bridges. These boys can knock a bridge together across a gully or a river faster than a Jap can stutter MMMMAAACCCCARTHUR." The slap at one racial stereotype, the enemy, at the expense of another, "these boys," was surely unintended, but is a subtle demonstration of the built-in prejudices of white wartime America.

AMERICA AT WAR 1944

Whether or not white and black women co-existed well in defense plants usually depended on the area of the country. In Eastern and Midwestern factories, firmly rooted racial biases held the upper hand to assure segregation, with the main objection for integration being white women's resentment of having to share the same rest rooms with black ladies. Female Californians, less traditional, co-existing in a more genuine melting pot, and more relaxed from year-round salubrious outdoor living, took a more liberal view. Yet, even in the upper South, like Frankfort, Kentucky, Rosies of both races labored together, like 21-year-old Bertha Stallworth, inspecting 40mm cartridge cases at the Frankfort Arsenal, and a co-worker behind her in 1943.

As in the rural South, black-white racial tensions in all urban centers were exacerbated by wartime conditions. In the former Confederacy, lynchings and floggings of blacks continued, as well as more subtle murders, and racially-motivated riots erupted near the new Army camps — especially where Northern blacks were stationed and treated to Jim Crow discrimination for the first time. In New York's Harlem, frustrated black youths committed so many crimes against whites that late in 1941 the city government began to investigate the causes. Two years later, fears over white police brutality against "colored people" (the most common white name for Negroes) led to rioting throughout Harlem in which six fatalities occurred. One nervous black store owner has erected these signs to protect his property from the black rioters. At least Harlemites enjoyed a man whom they facetiously regarded as their "great white hope" — the handsome, light-skinned Reverend Adam Clayton Powell, Jr. of the 14,000-member Abyssinian Baptist Church who married the superb boogie woogie pianist Hazel Scott and was elected to Congress in 1945. But the war was not kind to Harlem, where the colorful gaiety of its jazz spots and theaters yielded to the heavy mist of drugs.

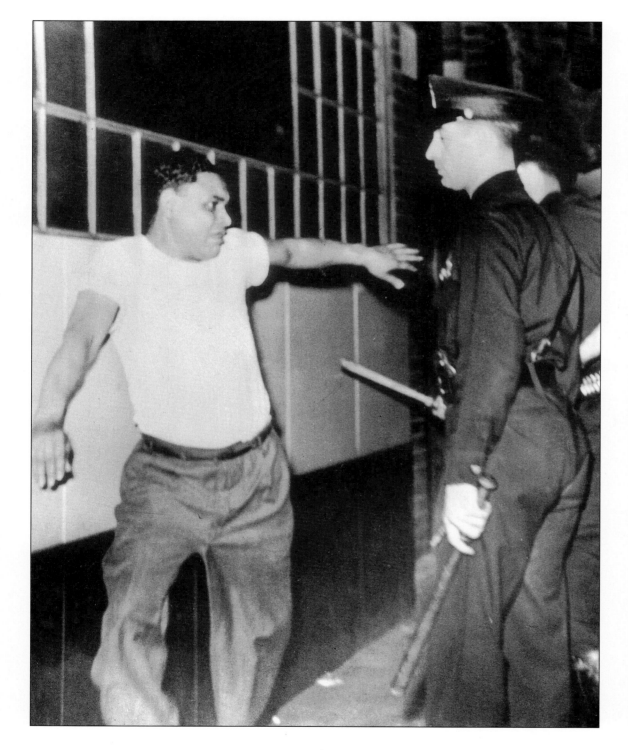

So packed was Detroit with native and migrant factory workers of nearly every race, creed, and color that an explosion was only a matter of time. It occurred on June 20, 1943, after a hot Sunday spent by tens of thousands of whites and blacks on Belle Isle, linked by a river bridge to the city. Incidents between petulant youths – many of them rejects from both industry and the military – flared up on the bridge and moved into the downtown area by midnight. Then, rumors spread through the filthy Negro slum (absurdly named Paradise Valley) that whites had killed some blacks, whereupon blacks began looting and pillaging white establishments – especially hated Jewish pawn shops. Whites retaliated, now hunting down and shooting blacks, who replied in kind. By daylight of the 21st the police had joined in – on the side of the whites, some of whom are seen overturning a Negro's car. Animal passions, lust for vengeance, and utter chaos descended over Detroit until federal troops arrived just before noon and restored order. All but nine of the 34 dead were blacks.

Terrified is the only word to describe this Negro backed up against a wall by Detroit policemen looking for weapons in the nighttime riot of June 20/21, 1943. In addition to the dead, some 700 persons were injured and over a thousand arrested. The official state and city investigations put the blame squarely on the blacks. But Detroit was only one battlefield of a nationwide war within the larger world conflict – the struggle of nonwhite minorities to be assimilated equally into a world conquered, shaped, and transformed by the inexorable march of Western European – and American – civilization. As the United States assumed the leadership over this new world during and after World War II, it would have to resolve the internal contradictions of its own democratic society. Whatever the travails of the future, the 13 million wartime blacks – 9 percent of the total population – did their part, including over 700,000 men in the Army, 165,000 in the Navy, 17,000 in the Marine Corps, 5,000 in the Coast Guard, and over 4,000 black women in uniform. The final victory knew no color.

1945

Victory in Europe – the long and short of it! But tall Coast Guard boatswain's mate Charles Fields and the shorter Sid Lukashewitz posed for this picture to convey visually the message in the caption: "V-E Day is merely half of victory. Both veterans of the Atlantic convoy duty on Coast Guard cutters, they will soon be fighting the Japs in the Pacific."

1945

AMERICA AT WAR

The year of Victory – in Europe (V-E) and over Japan (V-J) – began on Broadway with another hugely successful musical, *On the Town*, music courtesy of Leonard Bernstein. This was followed shortly by two more Rodgers and Hammerstein epics – *Carousel* on stage and *State Fair* on film. From the latter, "It's a Grand Night for Singing" reflected a jubilant America, which danced, sang, and cheered as the Allied armies, navies, and air forces finished the job of conquering Germany and strangling Japan into submission. Government curfews and relentless production up to the bitter end could not diminish the plain fact that Germany and Japan were finished. And though the great Roosevelt died, in the spring Yank and Red troops met in Germany as Hitler committed suicide, and the Americans went ashore at Iwo Jima and Okinawa while the B-29s pounded Japan. The Allies created the United Nations, and the Americans rang down the curtain on the titanic struggle in August 1945 by dropping the atomic bomb on Japan.

The American dream seemed to be finally realized, with a greater number of people well-fed, -clothed, and -sheltered than ever before and the message of democracy carried to every corner of the planet. The big swing bands, though yielding to small combos and popular singers, for the last time heralded the confidence and joy of the achievement, especially with the more modern sounds of Woody Herman, Stan Kenton, and Dizzy Gillespie, who was "Groovin' High" with all America. "My Guy's Come Back," rejoiced Rosie the Riveter as she gave up her war job to welcome him home, soon to begin the baby boom.

No-one would ever forget the historical drama in which all America had shared, yet one song at least ended the era with a very telling question, "Where Do We Go From Here?"

The new year began in gloom, as the massive German counterattack in the Battle of the Bulge scotched all tentative moves toward reconversion to peacetime, restored rationing, and kept most of the men from coming home. About all that teenaged gals and coeds could do was to socialize among themselves and wait for the men. This March 1945 "canteen fashion show" displays relatively inexpensive dresses which retailed between $8 and $13 – creations of one Grace Norman, who had perhaps been inspired by actress Billie Burke's radio program *Fashions in Rations*. The decor features samples of wartime teenage attractions – Cokes and donuts, Ping-Pong, "hep" slogans – including the ubiquitous "Buy War Stamps" – and girls dancing together; said the caption, "That's a mean Lindy hop those two chicks are doing" – the jitterbug step named for Lindbergh's 1927 solo "hop" across the Atlantic.

But as the Nazis were turned back from the Bulge by Allied armies advancing into Germany, more and more men were redeployed to the Pacific to fight fanatical Japan – where the fighting was expected to continue until maybe 1947. These men are being given a physical checkup at California's Camp Stoneman, which processed up to 4,500 men a day for embarkation to the western Pacific.

A grateful federal government had in 1944 granted the GI Bill to help returning veterans get established in civilian careers, while Army and Navy medicos lavished all that medical science could provide on the wounded. These six guys at Walter Reed Hospital's Convalescent Center in Washington are dolled up as "Amputettes" to display the Albert artificial leg. "All battle casualties," these Purple Heart recipients (the medal for being wounded) "prove what rehabilitation can do for a man with one or both legs gone," explained the February 1945 caption. A positive byproduct of the war were the major advances in medicine – from blood plasma to penicillin to artificial limbs and control of tropical diseases.

Military paranoia about a slackening of popular support and sacrifice for the war effort led to the decision by Jimmy Byrnes' Office of War Mobilization and reconversion to close all race tracks in January 1945 and institute a national curfew on all nightclubs and public places beginning February 25. Ostensibly, these midnight closings were explained as necessary to save electric power and the coal which generated it, although this was pure fiction. As Bruce Catton, a War Production Board staffer, later explained, "It was government by public relations carried to its logical and cockeyed extreme." In New York's Greenwich Village, the crowd at Cafe Society Downtown enjoys one last late-night highball as bandleader Phil Moore plays "Auld Lang Syne" on the piano and club owner Barney Josephson – arms around Moore – buys the last drink at 3:58 a.m. The totally unnecessary measure lasted only two months.

Not a German military train, this special Boston passenger car is filled with uniformed German prisoners of war just offloaded from a troopship for transfer to a POW camp in January 1945. American soldiers guard them at the rear of the car. These "krauts" don't appear very discomfitted by their situation, surely glad at least that they had not been captured by the hated Russians, who never even returned many Germans they had taken. Beginning in mid-1943, the British were glad to pass along several captured German generals to the United States, which placed them in a special stockade at Camp Clinton in Mississippi — 31 in all by the end of the war. German POW camps in America numbered in the hundreds, housing some 425,000 prisoners.

If the Pearl Harbor attack was the Great Shock of World War II for the American people, the sudden, unexpected death of Franklin Roosevelt on April 12, 1945 was no less shattering. A cerebral hemorrhage claimed him while relaxing at his Warm Springs, Georgia retreat. Thousands of people lined the way as the funeral train whisked the body to Washington for the funeral, then to the President's home at Hyde Park, New York. Here, the morning of the 15th, he is laid to rest. Eleanor Roosevelt is draped in a heavy black veil of mourning, her daughter Anna behind her. The grief-stricken nation remained in stunned mourning all three days for the man many had known as their only President. Columnist I.F. Stone reflected a week later that the nation had pulled through 12 years of repeated crises because of luck, "Mr. Roosevelt's leadership," and "the quality of the country and its people." For FDR "gave the United States...freedom from fear. Perhaps his most important contribution was the example, the superlative example, of his personal courage. Perhaps some of us will feel less gloomy if we remember it...."

The people stand in silent vigil outside the White House during the funeral, April 14, 1945. It was their quiet farewell to their leader.

AMERICA AT WAR 1945

New Yorkers dance in Wall Street on May 7, following an announcement by the Associated Press that Germany had surrendered. Alas, the bulletin had been premature, and the war in Europe went on. But Hitler had committed suicide, the Russians were in Berlin, Anglo-French-Canadian-American troops under Eisenhower had conquered western Germany, and the Nazis in Italy had just capitulated. So the smiles of these frolickers were hardly wasted.

New York's financial district – the "military-industrial complex," as Ike would dub it after its 20-year existence in 1961, that had beaten and destroyed the fascist dictatorships of Europe – stood for more than the immense wartime economic mobilization. Its achievement heralded the triumph of free enterprise, the very capitalistic system which the Depression had nearly undermined in the 1930s. America had never been stronger, nor had more people enjoyed the fruits of its prosperity ever before. Like a fluky day on the stock market, Wall Street could rebound from its missed cue on the end of the war in Europe and these ticker tape festivities. For that war only lasted one more day.

AMERICA AT WAR 1945

May 8, 1945 — after the premature festivities of the day before, New Yorkers now had it right. The Nazi scourge was no more.

New York World-Telegram
NIGHT
SURRENDER TO ALLIES
AND RUSSIA ANNOUNCED

The U.S. Army called upon James Montgomery Flagg, its veteran poster painter of both world wars, to grind out just one more – for the final attack on the Japanese Empire.

Stern reminders of the durability of the German war machine and the proximity of the threat right up to V-E Day, this submarine – the U-805 – surrendered off the coast of Maine. Surfacing on May 9, it had radioed its position to the U.S. Navy, which dispatched the destroyer *Varian* to accept its surrender four days later. A skeleton crew from the *Varian* is seen bringing the sub into the Portsmouth Navy Yard at Kittery, Maine on the 16th. Its emptied deck gun and antiaircraft guns are locked in the vertical position, and Old Glory announces the new owners. Three other U-boats were brought into the same yard, one having been en route to Japan with two Japanese officers on board; the sub's captain allowed them to commit suicide before striking his colors.

"WELCOME HOME, BOYS!" read the caption for this photograph of July 17, 1945. "Returning soldiers jamming the decks of the giant transport *Queen Mary* get enthusiastic welcomes from Red Cross workers filling the pier. The *Mary*, one of eight transports which docked in New York today, carried 15,642 troops, including 7,000 members of the Canadian First Army, who boarded special trains for Canada immediately after docking."

Wreckage from an A.A.F. B-25 medium bomber litters this hole in the outside wall of the Empire State Building at the 76th floor. On July 28, 1945 the Newark-bound plane encountered a morning fog over New York City, lost its bearings, and slammed into the north side of the world's tallest building. The plane exploded on impact and showered flaming gasoline onto adjacent stories, some of the fragments plummeting down the elevator shaft. All 13 crew members perished, as well as two soldiers and one sailor struck by pieces falling on to the street below. Several women office workers were injured and required emergency treatment. Note the people in the upper right hand corner inspecting the damage.

Down below, several New Yorkers survey a piece of the B-25 on the street while a policeman assesses the height from which it has fallen.

AMERICA AT WAR 1945

Democracy goes on at the grass roots level. At a town meeting in March, the people of East Kingston, New Hampshire vote 25 to 1 to support U.S. membership of the United Nations as proposed at the 1944 Dumbarton Oaks conference. Moderator John Hilliard and town clerk Mrs. Abbie Webster count the raised hands. New Hampshire was the first state in the union to vote on the plan. Even the man and woman in the street saw the importance of a new world organization to prevent another global war.

AMERICA AT WAR 1945

Hands across the table on May 2, 1945 symbolize the wartime solidarity of the United States and the Soviet Union . Secretary of State Edward Stettinius congratulates Russian Foreign Minister V.M. Molotov on his opening remarks before the initial session of the United Nations conference in San Francisco. This scene is clipped from a *News of the Day* newsreel later shown in movie theaters across America. Stettinius and Molotov headed their country's delegations. Americans knew the name of the Soviet commissar from the "Molotov cocktail" – a gasoline-filled bottle ignited and thrown by Russian partisans against invading Nazi troops.

Franklin Roosevelt had envisioned a postwar world dominated by the five "peace-loving" powers of the wartime alliances. Thus representatives of the "Big Five" met to form the U.N. at San Francisco, here discussing conference problems in Secretary Stettinius' apartment at the Fairmont Hotel on May 31: (left to right) Joseph Paul-Bancour of France; Britain's Earl of Halifax; Stettinius; Andrei Gromyko of the U.S.S.R.; and V.K. Wellington Koo of China. Russia was not yet in the Pacific war, but in August would both declare war on Japan and sign a defense pact with the Nationalist Chinese. The peacemakers did succeed in creating the U.N., but their nations would soon be involved in hot wars of oppression or liberation and in the Cold War between the two new superpowers – none of which had been anticipated by these delegates hoping for respite after the greatest conflagration in history.

V-J Day – Victory over Japan! This famous photograph caught an American sailor engulfing a gal in Times Square after learning of the Japanese surrender, August 14, 1945 (the 15th in Japan). Nationwide celebrations were now riotous as World War II had come to an end everywhere – officially on September 2 ,when the Japanese signed the surrender documents on board the U.S. battleship *Missouri* in Tokyo Bay. The *Missouri* was selected not only because it was Admiral William F. Halsey's flagship, but also due to the coincidence that it was named for President Truman's home state.

At Alamogordo, New Mexico, two key developers of the atom bomb meet at the exact spot where the test bomb had been detonated in July: Cal Tech physicist Dr. J. Robert Oppenheimer, director of the Los Alamos bomb project, and Army Major General Leslie R. Groves, Chief of the Engineers' Manhattan District, which superintended the bomb's development and production. Before them stands the melted base of the tower which had held the test bomb and the glasslike jade green cinders whose latent radioactivity forces the men to wear protective foot coverings. Their smiles of success belie the unspoken fears over the implications of their creation for the future of the human race.

The internal and external security of wartime America was represented by F.B.I. director J. Edgar Hoover (left), whose agents had frustrated Nazi-espionage and hounded dissidents, and General Groves of the Manhattan Project (center). With them, attending the International Association of Police Chiefs convention in Miami Beach, is Captain Donald Albury of the Army Air Forces, co-pilot of the B-29s which dropped the A-bombs on Hiroshima and Nagasaki, hastening the end of the war.

General of the Army George C. Marshall, wartime Army Chief of Staff, testifies late in the year before the Congressional committee investigating the Pearl Harbor disaster which had triggered America's official entry into World War II. Neither on this occasion or ever did Marshall explain why he had been out horseback riding and unable to be located that fateful morning of December 7, 1941. The United States had been asleep then, but never again. A Pearl Harbor syndrome would dominate American strategic planning for decades to come – fear that another sneak attack might destroy the country.

A new addition to the growing American population were war brides married to servicemen stationed overseas. Not until the war ended could these ladies come to their new home to settle. Thus, Navy "bosun" James McGuiness of Arlington, Massachusetts, welcomes his British bride Sheila after her arrival in New York aboard the *Queen Mary*. The baby boom was about to begin!

An unforgiving federal government was painfully slow to release the "COs" who had refused to contribute in any way to the war effort. This picture, taken 15 months after V-J Day, bore the caption: "The war is over for most folks, but these pickets demonstrate that war-time harshness still obtains for the conscientious objectors. Dressed in prison garb, they parade in front of the White House with signs urging President Truman to grant amnesty for some 700 still in prison, and for 5,300 others who have been released from federal institutions but remain handicapped by loss of their civil rights." The last would not be released until 1948.

What were the American people fighting for during World War II? This domestic postwar scene is the answer: life, liberty, and the pursuit of material happiness in a world free of aggression. A mother and daughter share the chore of doing the dishes in their comfortable Vermont home. But, of course, time did not stand still. Victory in the war was not only an end but a beginning—of a new era in which the American people had to win the peace and labor to realize the American dream: the greatest good for all the people.

AMERICA AT WAR 1945